W9-BBX-130

A Bouquet of Flowers

Inspiration Gathered from My Spiritual Garden

Esther Carls Dodgen

authorHOUSE®

AuthorHouse™
1663 Liberty Drive
Bloomington, IN 47403
www.authorhouse.com
Phone: 1-800-839-8640

First published by AuthorHouse 3/3/2010

ISBN: 978-1-4490-5142-6 (e)
ISBN: 978-1-4490-5147-1 (sc)

Library of Congress Control Number: 2009912384

Printed in the United States of America
Bloomington, Indiana

This book is printed on acid-free paper.

PREFACE

God has appeared in my life in many extraordinary ways, but mainly through the people who have touched my life and provided inspiration along my life's journey. My family, my extended spiritual family and my close friends have all been God's instruments in bringing me to this moment in time and to this stage of my spiritual development.

When I started this project I did not know what form it would take or what purpose it would serve. Nevertheless the call was as clear as the ringing of a church bell on a clear, crisp morning. Being given the opportunity to compile this anthology has truly been a gift from God. I have deeply sensed His abiding presence and guidance.

My sister and true friend, Ruth Werries, was instrumental in helping with photos, flower arrangements, and provided encouragement and input for the layout of the entire book. I am grateful to her granddaughter, Elisabeth Werries, who helped with the beginning of each chapter's design. I owe a special thanks to my literary advisors and supporters, and best friends, Ethelee Bunfill and Betty Hedrick. Jennifer L. Smith offered incisive criticism which helped tremendously.

I am grateful to Bill Loveland, Nona Neff, Duncan Locke, Anita Llewellyn, Mary Farmer, Carl Shinall, and my brother, Glen Carls, who were of immense help in finalizing the manuscript. The members of my Monday morning Bible study, my Sunday morning small group, and numerous others have contributed to this book in untold ways. I wish to thank them all.

The assignment has been completed. Now I dedicate it to all those who seek the cultivation of the combined inner and outer dimensions of their lives. My fervent prayer is that anyone who reads any portion of this collected wisdom will receive inspiration in finding clues to a deeper fellowship with God. May our lives be enriched by gathering a few of these spiritual flowers and sharing them with others as we journey together in His name.

Contents

Introduction

All seed-sowing is a mysterious thing,
whether the seed fall into the earth or into souls.
Henri-Fréderic Amiel (1821-1881)
Journal

This collection of spiritual writings can be compared to a flower garden sown with inspirational seeds gathered from many lands, from many ages, and from a great company of God's disciples from all walks of life. These seeds have been selected, arranged and planted in an order following my personal journey from darkness to light and subsequently, my attempts to grow in that light. They have sprouted, taken root, bloomed and become my own garden of inspiration. The flowers produced are of a very personal and devotional nature. Included in the compilation are selections of non-fictional prose and poetry from a wide range of writers in whose thoughts I have found a sense of real worth and a parallel to my own spiritual pilgrimage.

This experiential endeavor is an attempt to clarify my own journey toward God and to explore the formative influences of this journey. Thus what I offer in these pages are simply glimpses into my searching as a fellow pilgrim. This inner journey has to do with loving God and attempting to live in such a way that one's whole life somehow depends on perceiving and responding to His faithfulness.

Like the growth of the fruit-bearing tree, so is the growth of our spiritual life. After planting, the seed brings forth a tiny, tender shoot which bursts through the soil and grows into a sturdy tree filled with blossoms which must fade and fall before the delicious fruit appears. Similarly, our spiritual life begins as an initial turning of our heart to God with His great outpouring of grace, then develops and grows into a deep, sustaining life with Christ which produces good fruit—love, joy, peace, patience, kindness, goodness, faithfulness, gentleness, and self-control.

The fruit-bearing tree spreads its roots by quietly and effortlessly taking in nutrients and moisture from the soil. Its leaves soak up the sunshine and rains. Our roots, founded in God, spread far and wide as we take in spiritual nourishment and grow in the disciplines such as prayer, study, reading the Word of God and meditation. Our inner life soaks up this fellowship with God and with like-minded Christians and takes in the life-giving Living Water and Living Bread.

The fruit is a product of the sap that runs from the roots into the branches of the tree. The Holy Spirit in us is like the sap which runs into the branches. We, like the branches, live, grow and bear fruit, not by struggles and effort, but simply by abiding. This involves a complete surrender of the whole being to Christ, a constant looking to Him for grace. Strong winds cause the tree to be strengthened just as difficulties in life help us to develop resistance to this world's attractions. The cultivation and pruning processes involve periods of distress and waiting.

The development of this spiritual strength involves a growth which like the seed begins as something very small—His initial outpouring of grace, but with proper care grows into something grand and beautiful. The birds of the air come and perch in the branches of the tree just as others come and find shelter through our life in Christ.

This compilation is also an effort to capture the essence of basic spiritual truth. As we walk together on this inward pilgrimage and are illuminated by some of the great spiritual classics, it is my hope that you will find a vivid sense of an encompassing fellowship of those, from all the Christian ages, who have experienced the joy of knowing God. May we realize God's will for us to be one with Him and enter more deeply into that fellowship. The riches of all are ours to share and enjoy.

Let us light the flame of our minds from these words and draw from the refreshing waters of spiritual truth of these pages to help bring to fulfillment the desire for Him that He has placed within us and to learn those lessons of the abundant life that Christ so eloquently taught. May your life be enriched by gathering a few of these spiritual flowers, arranging them in your own bouquet and sharing them with others.

Part One

The Seeking Soul

Preparing the Garden

God has scattered all along the way flowers out of His own garden. Behold how the promises, invitations, calls and encouragements like lilies, lie around you! Be careful that you do not tread them under foot.

~William Harding (1792-1886)
John Bunyan

Chapter I

Sensing God's Initiative

The Seeds Are Planted.

Thine is the seed time:
God alone beholds the end of what is sown
Beyond our vision weak and dim
The harvest time is hid with Him.

~John Greenleaf Whittier (1808-1891)

God made us to have fellowship with Him. He is continually seeking us out, calling our names, promising to fill us with joy as we experience His love. We must allow ourselves to be found by Him. How can we experience God's love if we're not listening for His call? If we listen inwardly, we will hear His still, small voice inviting us to walk with Him "through the narrow gate that leads to life."

God Initiates The Encounter

God created humanity for a love relationship with Him. More than anything else, God wants us to love Him with our total being. He is the One who initiates the love relationship.

~Henry T. Blackaby And Claud V. King (contemporaries)
Experiencing God

*Jesus said, "But I, when I am lifted up from the earth,
I will draw all men to myself."*
~John 12:32

God formed us for His pleasure, and so formed us that we, as well as He, can, in divine communion, enjoy the sweet and mysterious mingling of kindred personalities. He meant us to seek Him and live with Him and draw our life from His smile.

~A. W. Tozer (1897-1963)
The Pursuit of God

What is more delightful than this voice of the Lord calling to us? See how the Lord in his love shows us the way of life.

~Prologue Of The Rule Of St. Benedict (6th Century)
Lines 19 and 20

*No one can come to me unless the Father who
sent me draws him, and I will raise him up at the last day.*
~John 6:44

If we are completely honest with ourselves we know deep down in our hearts that the usual goals and strivings of self-sufficiency and self-fulfillment we have are not our real destiny. We sense an uneasiness with the common, ordinary life of delights and pleasures and begin to hear with our heart's ears this quiet voice from the soul's depths a whispering of a more meaningful, richer life. We are in essence seeking God and feel that He is indeed drawing us to Him.

~Clara M. Matheson (contemporary)
Journal

The Son of Man came to seek and to save what was lost.
~Luke 19:10

The words of Jesus still echo down through the ages, "Come to me that ye may have life." The voice comes in many ways. To some it comes through the exquisite beauty of the universe and to others it comes as a call voiced in the needs of mankind, of human suffering. To another it comes boldly as he flees through the night of despair and denial with the Hound of Heaven on his tracks. Others hear the voice of God through the orderliness and unity of the universe. To some it comes in the quietness of God's house or in a moment of quiet devotion, through ceremony and stained glass and the spiritual moment of reverent music, a moment never to be forgotten. Others sense God's voice in sorrow or death. Still to others God's voice comes in the work of the home and in developing young souls in the quiet ways of love. In countless ways God calls us. Let us never think that one way is superior to another, and that therefore God calls one in a special way and not another.

~Catherine de Rambouillet (20th cent.)
Ramblings

Remember, he is the one who has identified you as his own, guaranteeing that you be saved on the day of redemption.
~Ephesians 4:30 (msg)

The call of God can never be understood absolutely or explained externally...What God calls us to cannot be definitely stated, because His call is simply to be His friend, to accomplish His own purposes. Our real test is in truly believing that God knows what he desires.... God is sovereignly working out His own purposes.
~Oswald Chambers (1874-1917)
My Utmost for His Highest

All the days ordained for me were written in your book before one of them came to be.
~Psalm 139:16

Not one of us has been left alone by God. We do our best to ignore Him, shutting ourselves up in our little cocoons, living unto ourselves as if He were not there, tapping on the windowpane of our hearts. Nevertheless we never quite succeed in shutting God out completely because we still yearn for that peace which only God can give. He is already showing Himself in our urge to seek Him.
~Clara M. Matheson (contemporary)
Journal

You did not choose me. I chose you, to go and bear fruit—fruit that will last.
~John 15:16

God does not always sound the trumpets before Him. He comes quietly, unobtrusively, in a casually begun acquaintance, in the communication of a seminal idea, in a book one happens upon, in a word dropped by a friend, in a gleam that flickers for a moment in the darkness and then vanishes, leaving behind a new hope that there is light and a sure path opening not far ahead. He sometimes comes in a disaster that makes one clutch at any straw only to find, by what seems sheer accident, one has laid hold upon a life preserver, in a demand, too great for one's own wisdom and strength and love, which spurs one to the last research that ends in the long-awaited discovery.

~Albert E. Day (1884-1973)
An Autobiography of Prayer

The Plowed Field Is Ready For The Seed

Begin to search and dig in your own field for this
pearl of eternity that lies hidden in it; it cannot cost you too
much, nor can you buy it too dear, for it is all; and when you have
found it, you will know that all which you have sold or
given away for it is as mere a nothing,
as a bubble upon the water.

~William Law (1686-1761)

Gold, even though you desire it, you may perhaps never possess; God you will possess as soon as you desire Him. For He came to you before you desired Him; when your will was turned away from Him He called you.

~St. Augustine (354-430)
Confessions

*For God so loved the world that he gave his one
and only Son, that whoever believes in him shall not perish
but have eternal life. For God did not send his Son into the world to
condemn the world, but to save the world through him.*
~JOHN 3:16-17

Who answers Christ's insistent call
Must give himself, his life, his all,
Without one backward look.
Who sets his hand unto the plow,
And glances back with anxious brow.
His calling hath mistook.
Christ claims him wholly for His own:
He must be Christ's and Christ's alone.

~JOHN OXENHAM (1861-1941), from
"Follow Me"

Closing Prayer

*Dear Heavenly Father, You know all about me.
You have a plan for my life. How wonderful it is to know
that you are thinking of me constantly. Help me listen,
hear and respond to Your call, Your invitation, Your choosing. It is
to You that I give all praise and glory.
Amen.*

Chapter 2

Realizing The Need For God

The Seeds Begin to Sprout

What an inexpressible comfort it is to know
that my Father is the gardener.

~James R. Miller (1840-1912)
Glimpses through Life's Windows

Fellowship with God is the deepest joy of human existence. He is our soul's necessity, our deepest hunger. We are not complete until we have this fellowship with Him. There is no possession or person who can give us meaning in our lives. We are generally unaware of the countless times He reaches out to us. He speaks and we don't hear. He appears and we don't see because we are often preoccupied with mundane things. The time eventually comes, however, when we realize how desperately we need Him. We were not meant for a life without God, and our immortal soul cannot be satisfied with anything less than God.

Our Deepest Need Is For God

He satisfies the thirsty
and fills the hungry with good things.
~PSALM 107:9

An immortal soul, from its very nature, cannot find what it needs anywhere save in God himself. True religion begins in the heart. It is not a mere set of rules to be obeyed—an example to be copied. It is Christ coming into the heart and dwelling there.

~JAMES R. MILLER (1840-1912)
Glimpses through Life's Windows

There is a God shaped vacuum in every heart.
~BLAISE PASCAL (1623-1662)
Pensées (Thoughts)

Who except God can give you Peace? Has the world
ever been able to satisfy the heart?
~GERALD MAJELLA (1726-1755)

If a man is not made for God, why is he happy only in God?
If a man is made for God, why is he opposed to God?
~BLAISE PASCAL (1623-1662)
Pensées (Thoughts)

In the deepest heart of every man God planted a longing for Himself, as He is: a God of love. No matter what we say, our hearts cry out for God to care, to be involved with us, to love us. This is His idea. He created this longing in us. It is the longing toward the "light that lights every man who comes into the world." The human race longs for love because the human race longs for God.

~EUGENIA PRICE (1916-1996):
Make Love Your Aim

Thou hast made us for Thyself, and our heart
finds no rest until it reposes in Thee.

~ST. AUGUSTINE (354-430)
Confessions

When therefore the first spark of a desire after God arises in your soul, give all your heart unto it; it is nothing less than a touch of the divine loadstone, that is to draw you out of the vanity of time, into the riches of eternity. Get up therefore, and follow it as gladly as the wise men of the East followed the star from heaven that appeared to them. It will do for you as the star did for them; it will lead you to Jesus.

~WILLIAM LAW (1686-1761)
A Serious Call to a Devout and Holy Life

He Is The Living, Eternal God

As the deer pants for streams of water, so my soul pants for you,
O God. My soul thirsts for God, the living God.

~PSALM 42:1-2

He is the great answer to loneliness. Without Him, we shall always be lonely, no matter what human friends we have. There is none other with whom we can be perfectly frank; none other to whom we can tell all ours sins and sorrows; none other with whom we can share all our hopes and dreams. Only God has the capacity to understand everything—to forgive everything—to make allowance for every error—to know why we did what we did—why we want what we want—why we fear what we fear—why we hope what we hope. Only God can understand in us all that we cannot understand in ourselves. God is the only one who in Himself can satisfy ourselves. God Himself, not what He can do for us, but what He is, is the answer—as water to thirst, as food to hunger, as truth to a puzzled mind, as beauty to the artist.

~ALBERT E. DAY (1884-1973)
An Autobiography of Prayer

The living God is at work in human history.
He is the one who loves and cares, who thinks and wills,
who created the world and who continuously acts within it.
He is never an impersonal force. He is the living God
on whom our lives depend. His reality is simply affirmed and the
rest of the Bible hinges on this great affirmation.

~ISABELLE BAKER (contemporary)
Unpublished Writings

God gave us this pressing inner need to find meaning in our lives. The encounter with the Living God is the greatest human experience possible. The circumstances and forms this encounter takes are infinitely diverse. It always comes as such a surprise that the conviction is inescapable that it is God's doing.

~CLARA M. MATHESON (contemporary)
Journal

Christianity is not a thing or speculation,
but a life; not a philosophy of life, but a Living Presence.
~SAMUEL TAYLOR COLERIDGE (1772-1834), in
I Quote: A Collection of Ancient and Modern Wisdom

Man needs Jesus Christ as a necessity and not as a luxury. You may be pleased to have flowers, but you must have bread....Jesus is not a phenomenon, He is bread: Christ is not a curiosity, He is water. As surely as we cannot live without bread, we cannot live truly without Christ: if we know not Christ we are not living, our movement is a mechanical flutter.

~JOSEPH PARKER (1830-1902)
The Inner Life of Jesus

Closing Prayer

*Is it possible that I have lived without You, O God?
Have I settled for less than real life, true satisfaction, and honest fulfillment? Can You be known? If I come, will You love me, welcome me, forgive me? I bow down now in humble acknowledgment of Your life-giving power. I want more—all of You, O Lord my God.
I pray in Jesus' name.
Amen.*

Chapter 3

Finding Clues Along The Path

The Tender Shoots Burst through The Soil

Abandon yourself to His care and guidance, as a sheep in the care of a shepherd, and trust Him utterly. No matter if you may seem to yourself to be in the very midst of a desert, with nothing green about you, inwardly or outwardly, and may think you will have to make a long journey before you can get into the green pastures. Our Shepherd will turn that very place where you are into green pastures, for He has power to make the desert rejoice and blossom as a rose.

~Hannah Whitall Smith (1832-1911)
The Christian's Secret of a Happy Life

Jesus came to show the way to an abundant life; a new way to think, a new way to act, a new way to live. He laid down his life for us, taking our sin upon the Cross. It is so simple—finding this true and fulfilling life. All we have to do is believe and receive His gift of grace. It can be received by young and old, wise and simple, sophisticated and common. Many people strive to find fulfillment in all the trappings of this world, never realizing that this only leads to a dead end. The gate of discipleship is too narrow to allow us to carry our worldly possessions with us.

Seeking With All Your Heart

You will seek me and find me when you seek
me with all your heart.
~JEREMIAH 29:13

If we would find God amid all the religious externals we must first determine to find Him, and then proceed in the way of simplicity. Now as always God discovers Himself to "babes" and hides Himself in thick darkness from the wise and the prudent. We must simplify our approach to Him. We must strip down to essentials (and they will be found to be blessedly few). We must put away all effort to impress, and come with the guileless candor of childhood. If we do this, without doubt God will quickly respond.

~A. W. TOZER (1897-1963)
The Pursuit of God

Grant me, O Lord, heavenly wisdom, that I may learn to
seek you above all things, and to understand all other things as they
are according to the order of your wisdom. Amen
~THOMAS À KEMPIS (1380-1471)
The Imitation of Christ

For with you is the fountain of life:
in your light we see light.
~PSALM 36:9

A rich man gave a feast, and summoned the guests. His call to them is the voice of the Spirit of the Father inviting all men to Himself. But of those invited some are busy in commerce, some in the household, some in family affairs—none come to the feast....He who cannot, and that altogether, decline the cares and gains of the bodily life, cannot fulfill the Father's will, because one cannot serve oneself a little, and the Father a little.

~LEO TOLSTOY (1828-1910)
The Collected Works of Leo Tolstoy

O, God, you are my God,
Earnestly I seek you.
My soul thirsts for you.
My body longs for you,
in a dry and weary land
where there is no water.

~PSALM 63:1

If God had wished to overcome the obstinacy of the most hardened, he could have done so by revealing himself to them so plainly that they could not doubt the truth of his essence, as he will appear on the last day with such thunder and lightning and such convulsions of nature that the dead will rise up and the blindest will see him.

This is not the way he wished to appear when he came in mildness.... Wishing to appear openly to those who seek him with all their heart and hidden from those who shun him with all their heart, he has qualified our knowledge of him by giving signs which can be seen by those who seek him and not by those who do not.

~BLAISE PASCAL (1623-1662)
Pensées (Thoughts)

I was wandering like a lost sheep, searching for You, O God, and I found You not, because I sought You wrongly. You were within me and I sought You without.

~St. Augustine (350-430)
Soliloquies

Small is the gate and narrow the road that leads to life, and only a few find it.
~Matthew 7:14

A spiritual kingdom lies all about us, enclosing us, embracing us, altogether within reach of our inner selves, waiting for us to recognize it. God Himself is here waiting our response to His presence.

~A. W. Tozer (1897-1963)
The Pursuit of God

But though we cannot by our own act lift ourselves out of the pit, we must by an act of our own take hold of the hand which offers us out of it.

~J. C. and Augustus Hare (c.1834-1903)
Guesses at Truth

To have found God and still to pursue
Him is the soul's paradox of love.
~A. W. Tozer (1897-1963)
The Pursuit of God

Jesus Is The Way

I am the gate: whoever enters through me will be saved.
He will come in and go out and find pasture.
~JOHN 10:9

The danger we have is that we want to water down what Jesus said to make it mean something that aligns with our common sense. But if it were only common sense, what He said would not even be worthwhile. The things Jesus taught are supernatural truths He reveals to us.

~OSWALD CHAMBERS (1874-1917)
My Utmost for His Highest

He shed tears for those that shed His blood.
~THOMAS WATSON (1575-1645)
The Art of Divine Contentment

Jesus is not the door into a little life. He leads us into the largest, fullest life…. To live for ourselves is to die. To make life an end in itself is to end life; to love your life is to lose it. But lose your life, and you save it; lay it down all at once, if God should so will, or a little at a time every day, for Jesus' sake and the Gospel's, and you will find it lifted up in power to draw men to Jesus.

~MALTBIE D. BABCOCK (1858-1901)
Thoughts for Every-Day Living

I am trying here to prevent anyone saying the really foolish thing that people often say about Him: "I'm ready to accept Jesus as a great moral teacher, but I don't accept His claim to be God." That is the one thing we must not say. A man who was merely a man and said the sort of things Jesus said would not be a great moral teacher. He would either be a lunatic—on a level with the man who says he is a poached egg—or else he would be the Devil of Hell. You must make your choice. Either this man was, and is the Son of God: or else a madman or something worse. You can shut Him up for a fool, you can spit at Him and kill Him as a demon; or you can fall at His feet and call Him Lord and God. But let us not come with any patronizing nonsense about His being a great human teacher. He has not left that open to us. He did not intend to.

~C. S. Lewis (1898-1963)
Mere Christianity

If anyone would come after me, he must deny himself and take up his cross and follow me. For whoever wants to save his life will lose it, but whoever loses his life for me will find it. What good will it be for a man if he gains the whole world, yet forfeits his soul?

~Matthew 16:24-25

Supposing one single man to have left a book of predictions concerning Jesus Christ as to the time and manner of His coming.... the argument would be of almost infinite force; yet here the evidence is stronger beyond all comparison; a succession of men for the space of four thousand years follow one another, without interruption or variation, in foretelling the same great event.... This is a case which challenges our assent and wonder.

~Blaise Pascal (1623-1662)
Pensées (Thoughts)

But these are written that you may believe
that Jesus is the Christ, the Son of God, and that by
believing you may have life in his name.
~JOHN 20:31

Jesus' Words Of Life

Jesus said, "I am the living bread that came
down from heaven. If anyone eat of this bread,
he shall live forever. This bread is my flesh, which
I will give for the life of the world."
~JOHN 6:51

Truth lies in character. Christ did not simply speak the truth; he was Truth—Truth through and through, for truth is a thing not of words but of life and being.

~FREDERICK WILLIAM ROBERTSON (1816-1853)
Sermons

The parables of Jesus are like great art. They express a profound simplicity. The familiar stories yield new vistas of thought each time they are explored. But you can never get all that is there.

~DOUGLAS BEYER (contemporary)
Parables for Christian Living

Jesus answered, "I am the way and the truth and the life.
No one comes to the Father except through me."
~JOHN 16.6

The words of our Lord shine by their own light, they carry with them their own credentials. Like the person who uttered them, they are unique. They are simple, yet profound, calm yet intense, "mild yet terrible." They have a peculiar force which expresses authority. They do not persuade or entreat or reason with the hearer: they penetrate, they convict, they reveal. The charm and the wonder of them are as fresh today, for the unlearned as well as for the learned, as when the people were astonished at His doctrine.

~ARCHBISHOP OF ARMAGH (1859-1938)
"Ruling Ideas of Our Lord"

I am the same yesterday and today and forever.
~HEBREWS 13.8

Closing Prayer

Lord Jesus, it is comforting to know
that I may seek You because You will be found; that
I may believe You because You are the truth; that I may
follow You because You are the way; and that I may
live in You because You are the life. Help me lose all ego and pride
and to release everything I have assumed important
so that I may enter through the narrow gate to
walk with You forever more.
Amen.

Part Two

The Pondering Soul

Watching in Wonder as the Plants Grow

I stood there in a lovely garden one night—
And marveled at the enchanting sight!
When Lo! There in the cathedral-like hush
I heard the swish of a painter's brush.
I saw the flowers and trees in prayer.
And knew that the Great Gardener
was working there!

~FRANCES ANGERMAYER (fl. 1950's)
"The Great Gardener"

Chapter 4

Perceiving God's Presence

The Shoots Grow into Sturdy Plants

> Some people, in order to discover God, read books. But there is a great book: the very appearance of created things. Look above you! Look below you! Read it. God, whom you want to discover, never wrote that book with ink. Instead He set before your eyes the things that He had made. Can you ask for a louder voice than that?
>
> ~St. Augustine (354-430)

God uses simple things and casual moments to reveal Himself to us, if only we had eyes to see and ears to hear. We can see Him in the sunrise and in the sunset, in the storm clouds and in the rainbow, in the smiles of others and in their tears. It seems impossible to sit under the stars on a clear summer night and look up and say there is no God. Or to listen to Handel's *Hallelujah Chorus*, and say that you have no feelings toward God! Throughout history countless souls have experienced a sense of God's presence with them that has brought absolute repose and confident calmness. Let us join the legacy of those who perceive God's presence in the world around them.

Opening Our Eyes

If we do not see him, it is not because he is not
here, but because we are spiritually blind.
~W. TALIAFERRO THOMPSON (1886-1964)
Christian Family Living

At autumn time God has dipped His paint brush in His palette of colors and splashed the hills and woods and fields with robes of saffron and crimson and gold and yellow and brown and scarlet. The sunsets are too gorgeous for human description. In this amazing garden of beauty our lips involuntarily sing forth the praises of the psalmist: "Bless Jehovah, O my soul: and all that is within me, bless his Holy Name."

~CHARLES KINGSLEY (1819-1875)

It is surprising how easy it is to hear music
in the waves and songs in the wild whisperings of the winds;
to see God everywhere in the stones, in the rocks,
in the rippling brooks and hear Him everywhere, in the lowing of
cattle, in the rolling of thunder, and in the fury of tempests.
~CHARLES H. SPURGEON (1834-1892)
Sermons

The light shines in the darkness,
but the darkness has not understood it.
~JOHN 1:5

There are joys which long to be ours. God sends
ten thousand truths, which come about us like birds seeking
inlet; but we are shut up to them, and so they bring us nothing, but
sit and sing awhile upon the roof, and then fly away.

~HENRY WARD BEECHER (1813-1887)
Autobiographical Reminisces

When God speaks, many of us
are like people in a fog, and we give no answer.

~OSWALD CHAMBERS (1874-1917)
My Utmost for His Highest

If God is present at every point in space, if we cannot go where He is not, cannot even conceive of a place where He is not, why then has not that Presence become the one universally celebrated fact of the world? The patriarch Jacob, "in waste howling wilderness," gave the answer to that question. He saw a vision of God and cried out in wonder, "Surely the Lord is in this place; and I knew it not."

~A. W. TOZER (1897-1963)
The Pursuit of God

The heavens declare the glory of God; the skies proclaim the work of his hands. Day by day they pour forth speech. Night after night they display knowledge. There is no speech or language where their voice is not heard. Their voice goes out unto all the earth, their words to the ends of the world.

~PSALM 19:1-4

Whenever the sounds of the world die out in the soul, or sink low, then we hear these whisperings of God. He is always whispering to us, only we do not always hear, because of the noise, hurry, and distraction which life causes as it rushes on.

~FREDERICK WILLIAM FABER (1814-1863)
The Life and Letters of Frederick William Faber

Can you sit on top of a hill in spring,
And watch the birds sailing by on the wing,
And see the clouds drifting in the sky,
And doubt there's a God who dwells on high?

Can you watch the butterfly flit through the air,
And see flowers blooming fragrant and fair,
Or watch the trees reaching ever above,
And doubt there's a God of wisdom and love?

~ESTHER ROWE (contemporary)
How Can You Doubt There's a God?

God is always here, wherever we are. But consciousness is so occupied with other matters that it is not aware of Him. Or consciousness is so dulled by its habitual occupations that it cannot perceive Him.

~ALBERT E. DAY (1884-1973)
An Autobiography of Prayer

This is why I speak to them in parables. Though seeing, they do not see; though hearing, they do not hear or understand.

~MATTHEW 13:13

Every mountain tells of his majesty and every crystal stream reminds us of the Water of Life. Each flower that opens pays homage to the Rose of Sharon and Lily of the Valley. His name is written in the splendor all about us and his voice is heard in the song of the robin or redbird as each new spring arrives. His glory is told in the fragrance of the jasmine and jonquil. The eagle on wing is a reminder of the heights to which we are invited. The music of the tossing waves and their pause at twilight are a part of his orchestra.

~ROSALEE MILLS APPLEBY (early 20th cent.)

We Begin To See

A state of mind that sees God in everything
is evidence of growth in grace and a thankful heart.

~CHARLES G. FINNEY (1792-1875)
Memoirs of the Rev. Charles Finney

The world around us is the mighty
volume wherein God hath declared Himself.
Human languages and characters are different in
different nations, and those of one nation are not
understood by the rest. But the book of
nature is written in a universal character,
which every man may read in his own language.

~JOHN WESLEY (1703-1791)
Letters

Have you ever risen early, climbed a hill, and watched God make a morning? It is overwhelming to listen to the music of heaven's choir as it sings of the majesty of God Himself.

~GEORGE MACDONALD (1824-1905)
Unspoken Sermons

This is my Father's world,
And to my listening ears
All nature sings,
And round me rings
The music of the spheres.

This is my Father's world:
O let me ne'er forget
That though the wrong
Seems oft so strong,
God is the Ruler yet.

~MALTBIE D. BABCOCK (1850-1901)
This Is My Father's World

When I see the sun setting in the West, as I saw it tonight—a beautiful center of red and about it a border of blue, just fading here and there into grey—I know that the hand of man did not paint it. When I look upon the gospel with its great answer, with its marvelous remedy, with its satisfactions for the whole nature of man, I know that it came from God—"Master, no man can do the work thou doest except God be with him."

~CLARENCE E. MACARTNEY (1879-1957)
Macartney's Illustrations

God and Father, I repent of my sinful preoccupation with visible things. The world has been too much with me. Thou has been here and I knew it not. I have been blind to Thy presence. Open my eyes that I may behold Thee in and around me. For Christ's sake, Amen.

~A. W. TOZER (1897-1963)
The Pursuit of God

God set before your eyes the things that He has made.
Can you ask for a louder voice than that?
~ST. AUGUSTINE (354-430)

For since the creation of the world God's invisible qualities—his eternal power and divine nature—have been clearly seen, being understood from what has been made, so that men are without excuse.
~ROMANS 1:20

Closing Prayer

Lord Jesus, how wonderful are Your works! You have so generously given Yourself to all that surrounds me. Forgive me for my inattention to Your continual Presence. May I become as preoccupied with You as I have been with me and this world. Let me see You, hear You, feel You in all I do and say, so that Your name may be glorified.
Amen.

Chapter 5

Recognizing God's Sovereignty And Guidance

The Flowers Are Planted in a Prearranged Pattern

O impatient ones! Did the leaves say nothing to you as they murmured, when you came hither today? They were not created this spring, but months ago; and the summer just begun will fashion others for another year. At the bottom of every leaf stem is a cradle, and in it is an infant germ; and the winds will rock it, and the birds will sing to it all summer long, and next season it will unfold. So, impatient Christians, God is carrying forward all the processes of your lives.

~Henry Ward Beecher (1813-1887)
Life Thoughts

Looking back, we begin to see that every moment in our lives has been planned. We can see it now—a letter received at just the right time, a chance encounter with a stranger, a sudden glimpse of untold beauty, a thought that came so forcefully that we knew it must have come from God Himself. Something was happening when at the time it did not seem so. It took place just as the seed in the soil was preparing to sprout and burst forth. Day by day we live knowing that all things are ordered by God to teach us what we need to know. At the end of our life, will we be able to say, "You sent me into life with a handful of seeds. Here is my heart, like a garden full of flowers."

All Wisdom And Power Are His

Praise be to the name of God for ever and ever;
wisdom and power are his. He changes times and seasons;
he sets up kings and deposes them.
~DANIEL 12:21

This is a piece too fair
To be the child of Chance, and not of Care.
No atoms casually together hurl'd
Could e'er produce so beautiful a world.
~JOHN DRYDEN (1631-1700)

I believe that the very existence of the amazing world of the atom points to a purposeful creation, to the idea that there is a God and an intelligent purpose back of everything.
~ARTHUR H. COMPTON (1892-1962), in
Knight's Illustrations for Today

On the one hand, we marvel at the immense size of the universe. On the other, God has made things so sub-microscopic that we can't even see them—the atom and its sub-components. He has made them with the same meticulous precision that He used in making the vast cosmos. In terms of size, human beings are between the size of a solar system and an atom. Would God skip us when He distributes His concern?

~JACK LOUSMA (contemporary), in
Scientists Who Believe

Oh, the depth of the riches of the wisdom
And knowledge of God!
How unsearchable his judgments,
And his paths beyond finding out.
~ROMANS 11:33

When men shout that "God is dead,"
they can only mean that He is not in the place where
they are looking for Him.
~W. A. VISSER, in
The New York Times, Dec. 20, 1965

We do not have to go to the universe to prove the existence of God from design… He is not far from every one of us. As Paul says "In Him we move and have our being:" and as Tennyson says, "Closer is He than breathing; and nearer than hands and feet." God is here. There is no escaping Him.
~CHARLES H. PARKHURST (1842-1933)

For the wisdom of this world is foolishness in God's sight.
~I CORINTHIANS 3:19

The doorstep to the temple of
wisdom is the knowledge of our own ignorance.
~CHARLES H. SPURGEON (1834-1892)
Morning and Evening Devotions

We are like clay jars in which this treasure is stored.
The real power comes from God and not from us.
~II CORINTHIANS 4:7 (CEV)

The humblest, simplest soul who has discerned the truth may know more of God than all the learned theologians.

~CLARA M. MATHESON (contemporary)
Journal

God does not show favoritism, but accepts men from every nation who fear him and do what is right.

~ACTS 10:34

In the kingdom of Heaven there is neither great nor small; all are equal. Those who look for something extra as reward for their goodness, are like the laborers who claimed a greater payment than that for which they had agreed with their employer; merely because in their opinion, they were more deserving than other laborers...No one can be higher or lower, more or less important, than another, according to the teaching of Jesus.

~LEO TOLSTOY (1828-1910)
The Complete Works of Leo Tolstoy

How great are his signs,
how mighty his wonders! His kingdom is an
eternal kingdom. His kingdom endures
from generation to generation.

~DANIEL 4:3

Changed Hearts Bring Changed Lives

The best that man can invent or discover is only a pale reminder of what God has done through the ages.

~ALEXANDER MACLAREN (1826-1910)
Expositions of the Holy Scriptures

I find the most convincing evidence of Him...in the quiet testimony of beauty, truth, love, goodness, peace, joy, self-sacrifice, and a consecration, which point to another kind of world within than one we see and touch.

~RUFUS M. JONES (1863-1948)
The Eternal Goodness: A Symposium of Faith

What an amazing fact stands out as one reads about the lives of men and women throughout the ages who have discovered the love of God and know his ever-presence in their lives. How can all these people be deceived? That is the miracle and the proof—changed lives of those who have given up everything to follow God.

~CATHERINE DE RAMBOUILLET (20th cent.)
Ramblings

Miracles are not in contradiction to nature.
They are only in contradiction with what we know of nature.

~ST. AUGUSTINE (354-430)
Confessions

Guided By A Gracious and Mighty Hand

If we believe that God is everywhere, why should we not think him present even in the coincidences that sometimes seem so strange?
~GEORGE MACDONALD (1824-1905)
Annals of a Quiet Neighborhood

You must remember that our God has all knowledge and all wisdom, and that therefore it is very possible He may guide you into paths wherein He knows great blessings are awaiting you, but which to the shortsighted human eyes around you seem sure to result in confusion and loss. You must recognize the fact that God's thoughts are not as man's thoughts, nor His ways as man's ways. And that He who knows the end of things from the beginning alone can judge of what the results of any course of action may be.
~HANNAH WHITALL SMITH (1832-1911)
The Christian's Secret of a Happy Life

It is God who works in you to will and to act according to His good purpose.
~PHILIPPIANS 2:11

What God arranges for us to experience at each moment is the best and holiest thing that could happen to us.
~JEAN-PIERRE DE CAUSSADE (1675-1751)
Self-Abandonment to the Divine Providence

Opportunities will present themselves to you as though by themselves. If you are simple in the presence of God, he will not leave you in doubt.

~FRANÇOIS DE FÉNELON (1651-1717)
Spiritual Letters

No one knocks at my door who is not sent by God.

~AUTHOR UNKNOWN

God touches our lives every day in order to form us into his likeness, slowly and silently, with so much gentleness that we are scarcely aware of it. Sometimes He does this by surprise or in a major upheaval in our lives. Time after time it has happened. As we look back we can see that God has indeed mysteriously led us to where we are.

~CATHERINE DE RAMBOUILLET (20th cent.)
Ramblings

God Made Us Unique For A Purpose

He determined the times set for them and the exact places where they should live. God did this so that men would seek him, though he is not far from each one of us. For in him we live and move and have our being.

~ACTS 17:26b-28a

Men go abroad to wonder at the height of mountains, at the huge waves of the sea, at the long courses of the rivers, at the vast compass of the ocean, at the circular motion of the stars, and they pass by themselves without wondering.

~ST. AUGUSTINE (354-430)
Confessions

There are no buds which can open without the sun, but there is a great difference in the time it takes them to unfold. Some have their outer petals so closely wrapped and glued together, that there must be many days of warm shining before they will begin to expand; and others there are which make haste to get out of the ground; and almost as soon as they are buds, they are blossoms. So it is with human hearts. Some are so cold and impervious that it seems as though God's Spirit never could reach them, and others there are which open to its first influences.

~HENRY WARD BEECHER (1813-1887)
Life Thoughts

We are not here by chance; God put us here for
a purpose. Life's greatest joy comes from finding his purpose
and doing it. We can try to find fulfillment and happiness in all kinds
of ways—money, pleasure, knowledge, fame,
power and so forth, but in the end we will discover that all these
things are meaningless, a "chasing after the wind."

~ISABELLE BAKER (contemporary)
Unpublished Writings

"For I know the plans I have for you," declares
the Lord, "plans to prosper you and not to harm you,
plans to give you hope and a future."

~JEREMIAH 29:11

God deals with us very differently. I have no doubt that on the other side we shall see that there is good reason why every one is what he is. When we evolve and come out we shall all be like flowers in a bouquet, which grow separately, and differ widely, but which when put together skillfully, are of equal importance. The large ones are no better than the small ones. The fine, dust-like blossoms fill up their own place, and are as essential to the perfection of the whole as any others.

~HENRY WARD BEECHER (1813-1887)
Life Thoughts

If the whole body were an eye, where would the sense of hearing be? If the whole body were an ear, where would the sense of smell be? But in fact God has arranged the parts in the body, every one of them, just as he wanted them to be. If they were all one part, where would the body be? As it is, there are many parts, but one body.
Now you are the body of Christ, and each one of you is a part of it.
~I CORINTHIANS 12:17-20,27

A man's highest pursuit is to find God's will for his life and then give his whole life to accomplish it.
~BERNARD HOLMES (contemporary)
Lectures

Closing Prayer

O God, how I love You.
Your glorious sovereign plan is so precious to me.
You have chosen this path for me. It is, therefore, a noble and sacred road. You know what lies before me this day. I am trusting You to lead my way.
May I not shirk from any sacrifice You may demand. Even though there is much I don't understand, I know You understand all, and I need have no concern.
Direct all my ways for Jesus' sake.
Amen

Part Three

The Awakening Soul

The Landscape Bursts Into Bloom

What the sunshine is to those flowers, the Lord Jesus Christ is to my soul.

~ALFRED, LORD TENNYSON (1809-1892)

Chapter 6

Accepting God's Invitation

First the Tiny Buds Appear

Those who have found God can only inspire others to keep searching. They can only plant the seed and hope the soil is right for the shoots to spring forth and the tiny buds to appear.

~Catherine de Rambouillet (20th cent.)
Ramblings

There are as many kinds of conversion experiences as there are people who have experienced God in a personal way. It is not a change we bring about in ourselves, but a change which God brings about in us as we permit ourselves to be filled with His love. Sometimes in a gentle and silent way we catch a glimpse of His Presence. Sometimes in a sudden burst of fire our souls are engulfed with God's goodness, and a new life is revealed to us. However it may happen, we open ourselves to God. His Presence takes possession of our hearts as He establishes His kingdom. We will never be the same again. Conversion begins with God and continues quietly within us throughout our lives.

Blind Eyes Are Opened

Open my eyes, that I may see;
Glimpses of truth Thou hast for me;
Place in my hands the wonderful key
That shall unclasp and set me free:
Silently now I wait for Thee,
Ready my God, Thy will to see;
Open my eyes, illumine me,
Spirit divine!

~CLARA H. SCOTT (1841-1897)
"Open My Eyes"

Suddenly, in the midst of great tragedy or joy, through windows hardly noticed before, we catch a glimpse of eternity, and begin to understand that all our life, all our achievement and glory, is as a grain of sand on an endless shore, a single bead in a chain that stretches on and on into infinity.

~SAMUEL DRESNER (20th cent.)
Three Paths of God and Man

The Word of God came unto me,
Sitting alone among the multitudes;
And my blind eyes were touched with light,
And there was laid upon my lips a flame of fire.

~HELEN KELLER (1880-1968)
"In the Garden of the Lord"

I pray also that the eyes of your heart may be
enlightened in order that you may know the hope to which
he has called you, the riches
of his glorious inheritance in the saints.

~EPHESIANS 1:18

This experience of God is the only thing which is certain and self-evident. Before his heart has been moved in this manner, a man is deaf and blind towards everything, even towards miracles. But once this interior sense of God has come to him, he needs no other miracle than that which has been accomplished within his own soul.

~ALEXANDER YELCHANINOV (1881-1934)
Fragments of a Diary

He may not be gotten by thought, nor concluded by understanding, but He may be loved and chosen with the true lovely will of thine heart.

~AN EPISLLE OF DISCRETION (14th cent.), from
The Cell of Self-Knowledge

My ears had heard of you but now my eyes have seen you.

~JOB 42:5

We require great confidence to abandon ourselves, without any reserve, to Divine Providence; but when we do abandon all, Our Lord takes care of all.

~FRANCIS DE SALES (1567-1622)
Consoling Thoughts

Amazing grace! How sweet the sound.
That saved a wretch like me!
I once was lost, but now am found,
Was blind, but now I see,

T'was grace that taught my heart to fear
And grace my fears relieved;
How precious did that grace appear
The hour I first believed!

Through many dangers, toils and snares
I have already come
'Tis grace hath brought me safe thus far
And grace will lead me home.

The Lord has promised good to me
His word my hope secures
He will my shield and portion be
As long as life endures.

When we've been there ten thousand years
Bright shining as the sun
We've no less days to sing God's praise
Than when we first begun

~JOHN NEWTON (1725-1807)
"Amazing Grace"

Out Of Darkness Into His Wonderful Light

Every story of conversion is the story of a blessed defeat.
~C. S. LEWIS (1898-1963)

I know that Christ is alive,
and personal
and real, and closer than we think.
I have met Him.
I have felt His presence.
~PETER MARSHALL (1903-1949), FROM
"The Tap on the Shoulder"

Throughout the ages God has revealed Himself to man and set aflame the fire of faith in his soul and imparted to him the truth that will set him free. Something remarkable has happened—something that is inexpressible and undeniable, something that makes life worthwhile. What a lovely expression of the difference that Christ makes in our lives: "who called you out of darkness into his wonderful light."

~CATHERINE DE RAMBOUILLET (20th cent.)
Ramblings

There is a remarkable, even exhilarating, variety in the way people describe their conversions. Conversion is a mystery of God, and the varieties of conversion experiences testify to that divine initiative seeking out those who are lost, finding them, and bringing them home.

~HUGH T. KERR AND JOHN M. MULDER (contemporaries)
Famous Conversions

I waited patiently for the Lord;
he turned to me and heard my cry.
He lifted me out of the slimy pit,
out of the mud and mire;
he set my feet on a rock
and gave me a firm place to stand.
He put a new song in my mouth,
a hymn of praise to our God.
~PSALM 40:1-3

In God's kingdom nothing is paid: everything is received. Everything is a gift, grace. His criteria are not our criteria. His ways are not our ways. Why me? We do not know. The one who worked only one hour received the same salary as the one who worked all day *(Matthew 20:1-16).* It was not a salary, it was a gift. To some He gives a marked sensitivity to the divine stirrings of the heart. Some who have hardly thought about Him, yet He comes to them in splendor and glory. Some sail smoothly along with hardly ever a turbulent wave. Others travel over a rough, rutted road with seemingly constant darkness. Each person has his own unique story. Only God knows the answer to the puzzle, but we know it is good.

~ISABELLE BAKER (contemporary)
Unpublished Writings

Spiritual awakening can happen at any time from childhood to old age, at any place—in a quiet moment in church or in a busy subway station, gradually or suddenly. We are all so different. God knows how to reveal Himself to each one in a special way, unique to his personality and station in life.

~CLARA M. MATHESON (contemporary)
Journal

Divine Moments Of Inspiration

What child of God is there who has not experienced at some time in his life those dramatic moments of divine intervention so soft and gentle, yet so forceful which make the heart thrill and reveal to it suddenly a world of peace, joy, and devotion? We become convinced of the absoluteness of the Divine and this inspires and molds every detail of our life. No matter how it happened it left us touched with an unknown power. We then knew that we were in the presence of the Lord. These experiences are memorable, life-changing and always unforgettable.

~CATHERINE DE RAMBOUILLET (20th cent.)
Ramblings

With joy you will draw water from
the wells of salvation.
~ISAIAH 12:3

You sit in prayer, perhaps reading the Scriptures, perhaps not. When in a secret instant, you unexpectedly yield your inmost Self to God as He receives you into Himself. In the moment of rediscovered union you silently cry out from the depths of your heart: "Why have I been so foolish not to realize that everything in me desires the fulfillment of the union with You and nothing else, absolutely nothing else. For this is what I desire to be. This is who I truly am—one marked, claimed and surrendered to Your love."

~JAMES FINLEY (contemporary)
The Awakening Call

In this world of sorrow and suffering there is a hidden and inexhaustible source of great joy of which the world knows nothing because those who have experienced it are unable to speak of it adequately. God's Presence can steal in upon us when we least expect it, often in times of crises, sometimes in the ordinary, daily routine.

~ISABELLE BAKER (contemporary)
Unpublished Writings

Often when a person is quite unprepared
for such a thing, and is not even thinking of God,
he is awakened by His Majesty, as though by a rushing comet
or a thunderclap. Although no sound is heard, the soul is
very well aware that it has been called by God.

~TERESA OF AVILA (1515-1582)
The Interior Castle

The day in my life when darkness became light will always remain a powerful memory. One summer Sunday when I was fourteen, as I was sitting in our little country church, there came over me a sense of bliss beyond anything I had previously felt. It was indeed, a "peace of God which transcends all understanding." My first thought was of God, of knowing God. That was the first decisive event of my spiritual journey. It was the first page of my lesson book, with many lessons yet to come. At that time I did not know what really happened, but now years later, I know that I was visited by the Almighty. It took place so quietly and forcefully that it has remained indelibly imprinted on my memory. I rejoice because that encounter that summer day during my youth has sustained me and inspired me ever since.

~CLARA M. MATHESON (contemporary)
Journal

As a child I was accustomed to spend many hours alone in my rowboat, fishing along the river, when there was no sound save the lapping of the waves against the boat....It was a time of watching and waiting for what I did not know—yet I always knew. There would come a moment when beyond the single pulse beat there was a sense of God's Presence which seemed always to speak to me. My response to the sense of His Presence always had the quality of personal communion. There was no voice. There was no image. There was no vision. There was God.

~HOWARD THURMAN (1900-1981)
Disciplines of the Spirit

It was in the year 1858 and I was twenty-six years old. I had just lost a precious little daughter five years old, and my heart was aching with sorrow. I could not endure to think that my darling had gone out alone into a Godless universe, and yet, no matter on which side I turned, there seemed no ray of light.

Then suddenly something happened to me. What it was or how it came I had no idea, but somehow an inner eye seemed to be opened in my soul, and I seemed to see that, after all, God was a fact—the bottom fact of all facts—and that the only thing to do was to find out all about Him. It was not a pious feeling, such as I had been looking for, but it was a conviction—just such a conviction as comes to one when a mathematical problem is suddenly solved. One does not feel it is solved, but one knows it, and there can be no further question.

I do not remember anything that was said, I do not even know that I heard anything. A tremendous revolution was going on within me that was of far profounder interest than anything the most eloquent preacher could have uttered. God was making himself manifest as an actual existence, and my soul leaped up in an irresistible cry to know Him.

~HANNAH WHITALL SMITH (1832-1911),
from her diary, in *The Unselfishness of God*

Closing Prayer

Compassionate Father, I commit myself to
You. You are the goal of my pilgrimage and source
of rest along the way. May my soul find refuge in the shadow
of your wings far away from the turmoil of this world.
May my heart find true peace in You.
Amen.

Chapter 7

Knowing God Personally

The Blossoms Pop Forth

I come to the garden alone,
While the dew is still on the roses,
And the voice I hear, falling on my ear,
The Son of God discloses.

He speaks, and the sound of His voice
Is so sweet the birds hush their singing!
And the melody that He gave to me
Within my heart is ringing.
~C. Austin Miles (1868-1946)
"In the Garden"

The whole experience of knowing God personally is a gift from God. It is unexplainable and incomprehensible to anyone who has not experienced it. When God enters our life, we become aware of something greater than ourselves. We realize that the only thing that really matters, that is absolutely necessary, is this new life in Christ. Now we see God as the center and all we do is determined by whether it will bring honor to Him. We become God's servants, serving Him in humbleness by showing love to others. How different this new life is when we discover all the little mercies of God which we never noticed before.

Everything Has New Meaning

To fall in love with God is the greatest of all romances;
To seek him, the greatest adventure;
To find him, the greatest human achievement.
~Raphael Simon (20th Cent.)

But those who hope in the Lord
will renew their strength. They will soar on wings
like eagles; they will run and not grow weary,
they will walk and not be faint.
~Isaiah 40:31

The moment man became aware of God and began even a slight fellowship with Him, that moment he knew what he had always wanted and what the answer to that want is. He knew too what the real meaning of life is—not self-fulfillment or anything that the self can create—but God, finding God, and finding oneself in God, and adoring God, and loving Him, and being loved by Him!
~Albert E. Day (1884-1973)
An Autobiography of Prayer

Whoever drinks the water that I give him will
never thirst. Indeed, the water I give him will become in him
a spring of water welling up to eternal life.
~John 4:14

The transformation may be so gradual that it passes unnoticed until, one day, everything is seen as different. Somewhere along the road a turn has been taken, a turn so simply a part of the landscape that it did not seem like a change in direction at all. A person will notice that some things that used to be difficult are now easier; some that seemed all right are no longer possible. There has been a slow invasion of the Spirit of God that marked no place or time.

~Howard Thurman (1900-1981)
Disciplines of the Spirit

Blessed is the man who trusts in the Lord
whose confidence is in him.
He will be like a tree planted by the water
that sends out its roots by the stream.
It does not fear when heat comes;
its leaves are always green.
It has no worries in a year of drought
and never fails to bear fruit.
~Jeremiah 17:7-8

The grandeur of God is surely found in His creation—in the subatomic world, in the heavens, and in nature. But unless we find the glory of God in His love and presence, we will miss His very best....The world of elementary particle physics has made me appreciate God as the brilliantly intelligent and powerful Creator. Personal contact with Him shows me what a loving God He is.

~Randall J. Fisk (Contemporary)
"Beyond Einstein," in *Scientists Who Believe*

If anyone is in Christ, he is a new creation;
the old has gone, the new has come.
~II Corinthians 5:17

Once one has encountered God everything is changed. One does not lead a charmed life---but it is amazing how charming the commonplace can become. One still has heavy work to do but one works with assurance and poise. One still has temptations to meet but they have been robbed of most of their power. One runs into adversity but the inner certainty remains.

~Albert E. Day (1884-1973)
An Autobiography of Prayer

Did you once drink at this fountain of living
waters, you would not seek elsewhere for anything to quench
your thirst; for while you still continue to draw from this source, you
would thirst no longer after the world.

~Marie Guyon (1648-1717)
Autobiography

We, like the psalmist, are pilgrims in a land not our own. For if we have found God—or rather, have been found of him—then we can never again really be at home in this world. Often, amid all the trafficking and low thought of irreverent and godless men, we too will feel the high pull of the mountains and yearn for the pure air of the sun-bathed peaks of God.

~Thomas H. Newcomb (20th Cent.)

This gladness in God is as a deep river; we
have only as yet touched its brink, we know little of
its clear, sweet, heavenly streams, but onward
the depth is greater and the current more impetuous in its joy.

~Charles H. Spurgeon (1834-1892)
Morning and Evening Devotions

The Goal Is To Know And Love God

Nothing else in the world is important except to love God and serve him with simplicity and joy.
~Thomas Merton (1915-1968)

The more one knows Him, the more one desires to know Him. And as knowledge is commonly the measure of love, the deeper and more extensive our knowledge shall be, the greater will be our love.
~Brother Lawrence (c.1605-1691)
The Practice of the Presence of God.

The chief end and duty of man is to love God and to enjoy him forever.
~*The Westminster Cathechism* (1648)

Every man naturally desires knowledge; but what good is knowledge without love of God?
~Thomas À Kempis (1380-1471)
The Imitation of Christ

If you keep watch over your hearts, and listen for the Voice of God and learn of Him, in one short hour you can learn more from Him than you could learn from man in a thousand years.
~Johannes Tauler (1290-1361)
The Inner Way

The vibrancy of our walk with God will depend upon the nourishment our spiritual lives receive. Spiritual reading creates a source of inspiration as it develops a curious, questing mind, a refuge or solace from the world. Reading can provide that single ray of light, that single link necessary to clarify and energize our whole mental and spiritual lives.

~CLARA M. MATHESON (contemporary)
Journal

Spiritual reading is, or least can be, second only to prayer
as a developer and support of the inner life.

~EVELYN UNDERHILL (1857-1941)
Concerning the Inner Life

The books I like the best are those
That give us more than what they say—
They simply open countless doors
Through which our thoughts can roam away.

~REBECCA MCCANN (early 1900's)
"Cheerful Cherub"

The one from whom you learn the most is not the one who teaches you something you didn't know before, but the one who helps you take a truth with which you have quietly struggled, give it expression, and speak it clearly and boldly.

~OSWALD CHAMBERS (1874-1917)
My Utmost for His Highest

The constant habit of reading devout books is so indispensable
that it has been termed oil for the lamp of prayer.

~HANNAH MORE

God's Love And Goodness Is Beyond Our Comprehension

Whoever does not love does not know God because God is love. This is how God showed his love among us: He sent his one and only Son into the world that we might live through him.
~I JOHN 4:8-9

God is beyond everything that can be understood.
~JOHN OF THE CROSS (1542-1591)

In my life everything had fallen. I stood on roll call in a concentration camp where 9,000 women died or were killed. In front of me stood a guard who used his time to demonstrate his cruelties. I could hardly bear to see and hear what happened in front of us. Suddenly a skylark started to sing in the sky. All the prisoners looked up and listened to the bird's song. When I looked at the bird I looked further at the sky and I remembered Psalm 103, "As the heaven is high above the earth, so great is God's mercy and love toward them that fear Him."
~CORRIE TEN BOOM (1892-1983)
Tramp for the Lord

The very soul and life of our love to God is His love to us.
~CHARLES H. SPURGEON (1834-1892)
Morning and Evening Devotions

I believe the greatest blessing the Creator ever bestowed on me was when He permitted my external vision to be closed. He consecrated me for the work which He created me. I have never known what it was to see and therefore I cannot realize my personal loss. But I have had the most remarkable dreams. I have seen the prettiest eyes, the most beautiful faces, the most remarkable landscapes. The loss has been no loss to me.

~FANNY CROSBY (1820-1915)

God has said,
"Never will I leave you:
Never will I forsake you."
~HEBREWS 13:5

We are able to have as much of God as we want. Christ puts the key to His treasure chest in our hands and invites us to take all we desire. If someone is allowed into a bank vault, told to help himself to the money, and leaves without one cent, whose fault is it if he remains poor? And whose fault is it that Christians usually have such meager portions of the free riches of God?

~ALEXANDER MACLAREN (1826-1910)

I consider everything a loss compared to the surpassing greatness of knowing Christ Jesus my Lord.
~PHILIPPIANS 3:8

God's love is unchangeable, and He
is just as loving even when we do not see or feel it.
~FRANCES RIDLEY HAVERGAL (1836-1879)
Latter Testimonies and Dying Words

No eye has seen,
no ear has heard, no mind has conceived
what God has prepared for those who love him.
~I CORINTHIANS 2:9

The Christian's life is a matchless riddle…Even the believer himself cannot understand it. Dead, yet alive! Crucified with Christ, and yet at the same time risen with Christ in newness of life! Union with the suffering, bleeding Savior, and death to the world and sin, are soul-cheering things.

~CHARLES H. SPURGEON (1834-1892)
Morning and Evening Devotions

You know everything I want to say before I start the first sentence. I look behind me and you're there, then up ahead and you're there, too—your reassuring peace coming and going. This is too much, too wonderful. I can't take it all in.
~PSALM 139:4-6 (MSG)

The man who has God for his treasure has all things in One. Many ordinary treasures may be denied him, or if he is allowed to have them, the enjoyment of them will be tempered that they will never be necessary to his happiness….Whatever he may lose he has actually lost nothing, for he now has it all in One, and he has it purely, legitimately and forever.

~A. W. TOZER (1897-1963)
The Pursuit of God

To the soul that is wholly bent upon God a thousand fretting cares and vexing problems which tear the lives of others in pieces simply cease to exist. With the submerging of the irrelevant, the soul is free to give itself to that which really matters.

~Emily Herman (1876-1923)
Creative Prayer

Closing Prayer

Lord Jesus, thank You that I can freely
approach You at morning, noon, or night at any time or place.
I am unable to understand the full mystery of Your Presence,
but I do know that You are near, revealing Yourself
to all who seek to follow You. Bread of Heaven, teach me
to find nourishment in Your Presence every hour
of the day. This is my deepest prayer.
Amen.

CHAPTER 8

Setting Out In Faith And Obedience

The Roots Spread by Taking in Nutrients from the Soil

> The aster has not wasted spring and summer because it has not blossomed. It has been all the time preparing for what is to follow, and in autumn it is the glory of the field, and only the frost lays it low. So there are many people who must live forty or fifty years, and have the crude sap of their natural dispositions changed and sweetened before the blossoming time can come; but their life has not been wasted.
>
> ~HENRY WARD BEECHER (1813-1887)
> *Life Thoughts*

Faith is the gift of God and He gives it to those who ask for it. You cannot argue or coax or reason or intellectualize to get faith. It is not something you learn. Your spiritual mentors are simply spiritual farmers who prepare the soil for the seed which God drops into the fertile soil. Faith in God gives us an awareness that there is more to life than basic material concerns. Pride also gets in the way. How can we know God if we think we already know everything and are filled with ourselves? "For it is by grace you have been saved, through faith—and this not from yourselves, it is the gift of God—not by works, so that no one can boast *(Eph. 2:18)*." Our faith and love lead us to obedience.

Faith Is The Gift Of God

Faith must be strong, or love will not be fervent; the root of the flower must be healthy, or we cannot expect the bloom to be sweet.

~CHARLES H. SPURGEON (1834-1892)
Morning and Evening Devotions

Men who stand on any other foundation than the rock Christ Jesus are like birds that build in trees by the side of rivers. The bird sings in the branches, and the river sings below, but all the while the waters are undermining the soil about the roots, till, in some unsuspected hour, the tree falls with a crash into the stream; and then its nest is sunk, its home is gone, and the bird is a wanderer. But birds that hide their young in the clefts of the rock are undisturbed, and, after every winter, coming again, they find their same places, impregnable to time or storm. Our foundation is the rock Christ Jesus.

~HENRY WARD BEECHER (1813-1887):
Life Thoughts

Every year I live—in fact, nearly every day—I seem to see more clearly how all the peace, happiness, and power of the Christian life hinges on one thing. That one thing is taking God at His word, believing He really means exactly what He says, and accepting the very words that reveal His goodness and grace.

~FRANCES RIDLEY HAVERGAL (1836-1879)
Latter Testimonies and Dying Words

A man cannot have faith without asking, neither can he ask it without faith.

~EDWARD MARBURY (17th cent.)

To be called to a life of extraordinary quality, to live up to it, and yet to be unconscious of it is indeed a narrow way. To confess and testify to the truth as it is in Jesus, and at the same time to love the enemies of that truth, his enemies and ours, and to love them with the infinite love of Jesus Christ, is indeed a narrow way. To believe the promise of Jesus that his followers shall possess the earth, and at the same time to face our enemies unarmed and defenseless, preferring to incur injustice rather than to do wrong ourselves, is indeed a narrow way. To see the weakness and wrong in others, and at the same time refrain from judging them; to deliver the gospel message without casting pearls before swine, is indeed a narrow way. Jesus Christ is himself the way, the narrow way and the strait gate. He, and he alone, is our journey's end.

~DIETRICH BONHOEFFER (1906-1945)
The Cost of Discipleship

Religious faith, when it comes to its true power,
does just that miraculous thing for us all. It turns water to wine.
It brings prodigals home. It sets men on their feet.
It raises life out of death. It turns sunsets to sunrises.
It makes the impossible become possible.
The master secret of life is the attainment of the power of serenity
in the midst of stress and action and adventure.

~RUFUS M. JONES (1863-1948)
New Eyes for Invisibles

Faith is believing what we do not see,
and the reward for this kind of faith is to see what we believe.

~ST. AUGUSTINE (354-430)

Faith is a work of God in us which changes us and brings us a new life from God. It makes us completely different people in heart, mind, senses, and all our powers, and brings the Holy Spirit with it. What a living, creative, active, powerful thing is faith! Faith is a living, unshakable confidence in God's grace. Through faith, a person will do good to every one without coercion, willingly and happily; he will serve everyone, suffer everything for the love and praise of God, who has shown him such grace. It is as impossible to separate works from faith as it is to separate heat and light from fire.

~MARTIN LUTHER (1483-1546)
Preface of the Letter of St. Paul to the Romans

Our faith awakens in us the awareness of God's self-giving love and thus sets in motion a reciprocity of love in moving us to give ourselves to God with all the loving abandon in which he gives himself to us.

~JAMES FINLEY (contemporary)
The Awakening Call

God often guides us through our circumstances. One moment, our way may seem totally blocked, but then suddenly some seemingly trivial incident occurs, appearing as nothing to others but speaking volumes to the keen eye of faith …They certainly are not haphazard results of chance, but are God opening up the way we should walk, by directing our circumstances.

~FREDERICK B. MEYER (1847-1929)

My soul finds rest in God alone; my salvation
comes from him. He alone is my rock and salvation;
He is my fortress. I will never be shaken.
~PSALM 62:1

Of all the prizes that earth can give
This is the best; to find Thee, Lord.
A living Presence near and in Thee rest!
Friend, fortune, fame
Or what might come to me—
I count all loss if I find not
Companionship with Thee!

~RALPH S. CUSHMAN (1879-1960)
Hilltop Verses and Prayers

Taste and see that the Lord is good:
blessed is the man who takes refuge in him.
~PSALM 34:8

Giving Ourselves To God

It's not the possession of extraordinary gifts that makes extraordinary usefulness, but the dedication of what we have to the service of God.
~FREDERICK WILLIAM ROBERTSON (1816-1853)
Sermons

The moment we make up our minds that we are going on with this determination to exalt God over all, we step out of the world's parade. We shall find ourselves out of adjustment to the ways of the world, and increasingly so as we make progression the holy way.
~A. W. TOZER (1897-1963)
The Pursuit of God

He will cover you with his feathers,
and under his wings you will find refuge;
His faithfulness will be your shield and rampart.
~PSALM 91:4

Wherever souls are being tried and ripened, in whatever commonplace and homely ways—there God is hewing out the pillars for His temple. Oh, if the stone can only have some vision of the temple of which it is to lie as part forever, what patience must fill it as it feels the blows of the hammer, and knows that success for it is simply to let itself be wrought into whatever shape the Master wills.

~PHILLIPS BROOKS (1835-1893)
Lectures

Give up yourself to God without reserve; in
singleness of heart, meeting everything that every
day brings forth, as something that comes from God.

~WILLIAM LAW (1686-1761)
A Serious Call to a Devout and Holy Life

If anyone is thirsty, let him come to me
and drink. Whoever believes in me, as the Scripture
has said, streams of living water will flow from within him.
By this he meant the Spirit, Whom those who believed
in him were later to receive.
~JOHN 7:37-39

Take, Lord, all my liberty, my memory,
my understanding, and my whole will. You have given
me all that I have, all that I am, and I surrender all to your divine
will. Give me only your love and your grace. With this
I am rich enough, and I have no more to ask.
~IGNATIUS OF LOYOLA (1491-1556)

Growing Spiritually Is A Lifetime Adventure

The living of the spiritual life
is not the decision of a moment;
It is the achievement of a lifetime,
enabled and empowered by the Holy Spirit.
~BERNARD CHRISTENSON (20th cent.)

Grow in the grace and knowledge of our Lord and
Savior Jesus Christ. To him be glory both now and forever.
~II PETER 3:18

Unless a tree has produced blossoms in spring
you will vainly look for fruit in autumn.
~AUGUSTUS W. HARE (1834-1903)
Guesses at Truth

To become Christ-like is the only thing in the whole
world worth caring for, the thing before which every ambition of
man is folly and all lower achievement vain.
~HENRY DRUMMOND (1851-1897)
The Greatest Thing in the World

*Whatever you do, whether in deed or word,
do it all in the name of the Lord Jesus, giving thanks to
God the Father through him.*
~COLOSSIANS 3:17

The true purpose of all spiritual disciplines is to clear away whatever may block our awareness of that which is God in us. The aim is to get rid of whatever may so distract the mind and encumber the life.
~HOWARD THURMAN (1900-1981)
Disciplines of the Spirit

*He who began a good work in you will carry it on to
completion until the day of Christ Jesus.*
~PHILIPPIANS 1:6

Little self-denials, little passing words of sympathy,
little nameless acts of kindness, little silent victories over favorite
temptations—these are the silent threads of gold which,
when woven together, gleam out so brightly
in the pattern of life that God approves.
~FREDERICK W. FARRAR (1831-1903)

To have found God is not an end in itself, but a beginning.
~FRANZ ROSENSWEIG (1886-1929)

To grow as do the lilies means an interior abandonment of the rarest kind. We are to be infinitely passive regarding ourselves, but infinitely active with regard to our attention and response to God. Self must step aside to let God do the work. Maybe you feel yourself planted in a desert soil where nothing can grow. Even so, trust fully in God, the divine Husbandman. He will make the very desert blossom as the rose and you "shall be as a tree planted by the waters…and shall not see when heat cometh…neither shall cease from yielding fruit."

~HANNAH WHITALL SMITH (1832-1911)
The Christian's Secret of a Happy Life

To discover God in the smallest
and most ordinary things, as well as in the
greatest, is to possess a rare and sublime faith.

~JEAN-PIERRE DE CAUSSADE (1675-1751)
Self Abandonment to the Divine Providence

Jesus replied, "Love the Lord your God with all your heart, and with all your soul, and with all your strength and with all your mind; This is the first and greatest commandment. And the second is like it: Love your neighbor as yourself. All the Law and the Prophets hang on these two commandments."

~MATTHEW 22:37-40

Obedience—First And Foremost

Obedience is not an option.
It is required of every servant.

~HENRY T. BLACKABY AND CLAUDE V. KING (contemporaries)
Experiencing God

*Whoever has my commands and obeys them,
he is the one who loves me. He who loves me will be loved by my Father, and I too will love him and show myself to him.*
~JOHN 14:21

No virtue can surpass obedience in its ministry to the life with God. It is the condition of all other virtues. No one who is disobedient can be pure or truthful or just or generous. Everyone who has learned to obey is more certain to acquire all the other qualities that equip the soul for companionship with God.

~ALBERT E. DAY (1884-1973)
Discipline and Discovery

*Jesus learned obedience from what he suffered,
and, once made perfect, he became
the source of eternal salvation for all who obey him.*
~HEBREWS 5:8b-9

Wait for the Lord and keep his way *(Psalm 37:34a).* This is pure and simply dependence upon God, not delay, as we sometimes think. "Waiting" here does not mean to sit around and do nothing, but to expect. God has spoken. We are to do.

~CLARA M. MATHESON (contemporary)
Journal

Practice the disciplines but do not keep score. Practice and forget. Never, never compare your record with that of any other person in the world. You're not out to break any records but to break the hold things and people and the ego have upon your attention.

~ALBERT E. DAY (1884-1973)
Discipline and Discovery

*I will show you what he is like who comes
to me and hears my words and puts them into practice.
He is like a man building a house, who dug down deep and
laid the foundation on rock. When a flood came, the torrent struck
that house but could not shake it, because it was well built. But the
one who hears my words and does not put them to practice is like a
man who built a house on the ground without a foundation. The
moment the torrent struck that house, it collapsed
and its destruction was complete.*

~LUKE 6:47-49

To be a servant of God means to have a great charity toward one's neighbor and an unshakable resolution to follow the Divine Will in all things, trusting in God with simplicity and humility, bearing with one's defects and patiently tolerating the imperfection of others.

~FRANCIS DE SALES (1567-1622)
Introduction to the Devout Life

*Anyone who listens to the word but does
not do what it says is like a man who looks at his
face in the mirror and, after looking at himself, goes away and
immediately forgets what he looks like.*

~JAMES 1:23

Closing Prayer

*Grant me, O Lord, to know what is worth
knowing and to love what is worth loving. Do not let
me judge by what I see, nor pass sentence according to what
I hear, but to judge right between things that differ.*

~THOMAS À KEMPIS (1380-1471)
The Imitation of Christ

Part Four

The Joyful Soul

Enjoying the Garden

Every soul that is truly alive has a garden of which no other holds the key; and in hours of weariness, when it is breathless with the hot race of life, and harassed by a babble of voices, it slips through the gate and walks at peace among the flowers. There is a garden of the world where Jesus walks and the clash of the world cannot drown the music of His voice.

~EMILY HERMAN (1876-1923)
The Secret Garden of the Soul

Chapter 9

Discovering Inner Peace

The Branches Grow and Bear Fruit

Contentment is one of the flowers of heaven, and if we would have it, it must be cultivated; it will not grow in us by nature; it is the new nature alone that can produce it.

~Charles H. Spurgeon (1834-1892)
Morning and Evening Devotions

If we look upon everything as being under God's influence, life will become increasingly full of joy. No life can be dull when there is a watchful anticipation of glad surprise and wonder concerning how God will use seemingly little incidents in our lives to His glory. This is not the flamboyant, outward manifestation of worldly happiness. It is the deep assurance that Christ has claimed us for all eternity. Joy is a very elusive thing, yet it can be found in the simplest places. It is always knocking on our door, but we do not recognize it. It is not free, yet we cannot buy it. It comes on bird's wings as we go about our lives serving our Master in simple ordinary ways.

Joy Is God's Abundant Life Echoing Within Us

You have made known to me the path of life;
you will fill me with joy in your presence, with eternal
pleasures at your right hand.
~PSALM 16:11

Joy is distinctly a Christian word and Christian thing. It is the reverse of happiness. Happiness is the result of what happens of an agreeable sort. Joy has its springs deep down inside. And that spring never runs dry, no matter what happens. Only Jesus gives that joy. He had joy, singing its music within, even under the shadow of the cross.

~SAMUEL DICKEY GORDON (1859-1936)
Quiet Talks: Selections from S. D. Gordon

Joy is neither within us only, nor without us;
it is the union of ourselves with God.
~BLAISE PASCAL (1623-1662)
Pensées (Thoughts)

When asked why his music was always so full of gladness, Franz Joseph Haydn answered, "I cannot make it otherwise. I write according to the thoughts I feel. When I think upon my God, my heart is so full of joy that the notes dance and leap from my pen."

~FRANZ JOSEPH HAYDN (1732-1809), in
The Spiritual Lives of Great Composers

Though you have not seen him, you love him;
and even though you do not see him now, you believe in him and are filled with an inexpressible and glorious joy.
~I PETER 1:8

Do not look for rest in any pleasure, because you were not created for pleasure: you were created for JOY. And if you do not know the difference between pleasure and joy, you have not yet begun to live. Life in this world is full of pain. But pain, which is the contrary of pleasure, is not necessarily the contrary of happiness or of joy.
~THOMAS MERTON (1915-1968)
Seeds of Contemplation

Joy is the most infallible sign of the presence of God.
~LEON BLOY (1848-1917)

Joy is not something we can achieve by pursuing it. It is rather something born in the heart of the one who has found companionship with God and which overflows into a life in harmony with God. Regardless of outer circumstances, wealth or poverty, health or sickness, it visits the souls of those who are committed in their journey with Him.
~CATHERING DE RAMBOUILLET (20th cent.)
Ramblings

Joy is the flag flying over the citadel of the soul
indicating that the King is in residence.
~Author Unknown

Joy is primarily a discovery of the soul, when God makes known his presence, where there are no words, no outward song, only the Divine Movement. This is the joy that the world cannot give. This is the joy that keeps watch against all the emissaries of sadness of mind and weariness of soul. This is the joy that comforts and is the companion, as we walk even through the valley of the shadow of death.

~HOWARD THURMAN (1900-1981)
Disciplines of the Spirit

You will go out in joy
and be led forth in peace;
the mountains and hills
will burst into song before you,
and all the trees of the field
will clap their hands.
~ISAIAH 55:12

Happiness Is A By-Product Of Love

Happiness is the greatest paradox in nature. It can grow in any soil, live under any conditions. It defies environment. The reason for this is that it does not come from without but from within. Whenever you see a person seeking happiness outside himself, you can be sure he has never yet found it.

~FORMAN LINCICOME (1879-1960)

The Beatitudes are the essence of the Gospel message. They tell what happens to people who embrace Jesus' teachings. They sum up what happiness is and how it is obtained. They are so comprehensive that one could almost say that the rest of the Gospels simply elaborate upon them and show how they can be carried out in the daily lives of His followers. The Beatitudes suggest that happiness is a by-product of other things such as humility, simplicity, purity of heart, mercy, peace-making, and being persecuted because of righteousness.

~CLARA M. MATHESON (contemporary)
Journal

A happy life is not built up of tours abroad
and pleasant holidays, but of little clumps of violets noticed
by the roadside, hidden away almost so that only those can see them
who have God's peace and love in their hearts; in one long
continuous chain of little joys, little whispers from the
spiritual world, and little gleams of sunshine
on our daily work.

~EDWARD ADRIAN WILSON (1872-1912)

The world has its own idea of blessedness. Blessed is the man who is always right. Blessed is the man who is satisfied with himself. Blessed is the man who is strong. Blessed is the man who rules. Blessed is the man who is rich. Blessed is the man who is popular. Blessed is the man who enjoys life. These are the beatitudes of sight and of this present world. It comes with a shock and opens a new realm of thought, that no one of these men entered Jesus' mind when He talked of blessedness. "Blessed," said Jesus, "is the man who thinks lowly of himself; who has passed through great trials; who gives in and endures; who longs for perfection; who carries a tender heart; who has a passion for holiness; who sweetens human life; who dares to be true to conscience."

~JOHN WATSON (1575-1645)

Abiding In God's Peace

We are not at peace with others because we are not at peace with ourselves, and we are not at peace with ourselves because we are not at peace with God.

~THOMAS MERTON (1915-1968)

Our souls may lose their peace and even disturb other people's if we are always criticizing trivial actions which often are not real defects at all, but we construe them wrongly through ignorance of their motives.

~TERESA OF AVILA (1515-1582)
The Ways of Perfection

Peace I leave with you; my peace I give you.
I do not give to you as the world gives.
Do not let your hearts be troubled and do not be afraid.

~JOHN 14:27

Peace does not dwell in outward things, but within the soul; we may preserve it in the midst of the bitterest pain, if our will remain firm and submissive. Peace in this life springs from acquiescence, not in an exemption from suffering.

~FRANÇOIS DE FÉNELON (1651-1715)
Letters

He alone is truly wealthy and lacks nothing who knows how to be content with what he has….in the conviction that whatever God desires for him or leads him to is better than he understands.

~JOHN A. COMENIUS (1592-1670)
The Labyrinth of the World

Let the peace of Christ rule in your hearts, since as members of one body you were called to peace.
~COLOSSIANS 3:11

In Cicero and Plato, and other such writers, I meet with many things acutely said, and things that excite a certain warmth of emotions, but in none of them do I find these words, 'Come unto me, all ye that labor, and are heavy laden, and I will give you rest.'
~ST. AUGUSTINE (354-430)
Confessions

The man who wishes to prove himself always
in the right, in everything that he does, sees, hears and
discusses, and who will not give way and be
silenced, will never be at peace in himself.
~JOHANNES TAULER (1290-1361
The Inner Man

You will keep in perfect peace
him whose mind is steadfast, because he trusts in you.
~ISAIAH 26:3

The Christian has a deep, silent, hidden peace, which the world sees not—like some well in a retired and shady place.
~JOHN HENRY NEWMAN (1801-1890)
Parochial and Plain Sermons

Those who know nothing of the spiritual life declare that it is impossible to experience real peace and heavenly joy in this grief-stricken world. But those who have experience of the spiritual life know that just as one finds here and there in the midst of the ice fields of the polar regions flowing streams of hot water, so in the midst of this cold and sorrow-laden world there are to be found flowing in the hearts of believers restful streams of heavenly peace, for hidden fire of the Holy Spirit glows within them.

~SADHU SUNDAR SINGH (1889-1929)
At the Master's Feet

The fewer desires, the more peace.

~THOMAS WILSON (1663-1753):
Maxims of Piety and Christianity

To discover God in the smallest and most ordinary things, as well as in the greatest, is to possess a rare and sublime faith. To find contentment in the present moment is to relish and adore the divine will in the succession of all the things to be done and suffered which make up the duty to the present moment!

~JEAN-PIERRE DE CAUSSADE (1675-1751)
Sacrament of the Present Moment

I will lie down and sleep in peace,
for you alone, O Lord,
make me dwell in peace.
~PSALM 4:8

Having The Mind Of Christ

Do not conform any longer to the pattern
of this world, but be transformed by the renewing of your minds.
~ROMANS 12:2

Our minds, like our bodies, grow by what they take in. If we desire success and money, we become unfeeling and inhuman. If we desire God above all things, we become a part of God and his abundance.

~CLARA M. MATHESON (contemporary)
Journal

We all know that our state of mind affects our seeing. If we are to see God and God's children as Christ would have us see them, we must use the eyes of the heart.

~RALPH W. SOCKMAN (1889-1970)
The Higher Happiness

Two men looked through prison bars—
One saw mud, the other stars.

~AUTHOR UNKNOWN

Your living is determined not so much by what life brings to you as by the attitude you bring to life; not so much by what happens to you as by the way your mind looks at what happens. Circumstances and situations do color life, but you have been given the mind to choose what the color shall be.

~JOHN H. MILLER (20th cent.)

So we fix our eyes not on what is seen, but on what is unseen. For what is seen is temporary, but what is unseen is eternal.

~II CORINTHIANS 4:18

He who wants to be the friend of Christ must forsake much
that the world counts friendship; he who desires
to see God must close his eyes to many things which
the world thinks desirable; and he who wishes
to hear the voice of the Spirit must stop his ears against
the babble of tongues and put a seal upon his lips.
~EMILY HERMAN (1876-1923)
Creative Prayer

Give your entire attention to what God is doing right now, and don't get worked up about what may or may not happen tomorrow. God will help you deal with whatever hard things come up when the time comes.
~MATTHEW 6:4 (MSG)

Our attitude to life is always a reflection of our attitude to God.
~PAUL TOURNIER (1889-1986)
The Adventure of Living

Closing Prayer

Grant me, O Lord, the inward happiness
and the serenity which comes from living close to You.
Renew in me daily the sense of joy and let the Eternal Spirit of
the Father dwell in my soul and body, filling every
corner of my heart with light and grace, so that
I may bear witness to the Light, giving
You thanks always for all things.
Amen.

Chapter 10

Valuing Strength In Quietness And Trust

The Fruit Is a Product of the Sap Running from the Roots to the Branches.

> Quietness and stillness bring the dew. At night when the leaves and grass are still, the plants' pores are open to receive the refreshing and invigorating bath. And spiritual dew comes from quietly lingering in the Master's presence.
>
> ~Dr. Pardington (18th cent.)

The great matters of life may blossom in activity, but they are rooted in silence. God comes to us when there is a silence within us. Silence is listening with all our might to God. This is prayer at its best. We must learn to be still, to listen and to turn our soul to the practice of silent communion with God. Activity and busyness often hide God's voice. We get away from rumors and judgments as we close our minds to what the world thinks is desirable, so we can sense the Spirit. We begin to know the power of prayer. Silence will begin to speak loudly, and we will not be able to ignore the voice of God calling to us.

Appreciating Solitude

Be still and know that I am God.
~PSALM 46:10

Inner stillness is an absolute necessity to truly knowing God.
~HANNAH WHITALL SMITH (1832-1911)
The Secret of a Happy Life

We can cultivate an inner solitude and silence that sets us free from loneliness and fear. Loneliness is inner emptiness. Solitude is inner fulfillment. Solitude is not first a place but a state of mind and heart. There is a solitude of the heart that can be maintained at all times. Crowds or the lack of them have little to do with this inward attentiveness.... In the midst of noise and confusion we are settled into a deep inner silence. The purpose of silence and solitude is to be able to see and hear. Control rather than no noise is the key to silence.

~TERESA OF AVILA (1515-1582)
Interior Castle

You can force a rose bud open, but you spoil the flower.
Leave everything to Him, without exception. "Not what I will,
but what you will" *(Mark 14: 36)*
~STEPHEN MERRIT (19th cent.)

It is in the desert that the dew
is freshest and the air is the most pure.
~ANDREW BONAR (1810-1892)

Deserts, silence, solitudes are "not necessarily places but states of mind and heart." These deserts can be found in the midst of the city, and in the everyday of our lives. We need only to look for them and realize our tremendous need for them. They will be small solitudes, little deserts, tiny pools of silence, but the experience they will bring, if we are disposed to enter them, may be as exultant and holy as all the deserts of the world, even the one God himself entered.

~CATHERINE DE HUECK DOHERTY (1896-1985)
Foustinia

Anyone can retire into a quiet place, but it's the shutting of the door that makes the difference.

~EVELYN UNDERHILL (1857-1941)
Fruits of the Spirit

We have been fooled by the crowd saying that activities, noise, size and programs lead us to God. Often when we are alone, without people to talk to, books to read and television to watch, we become uneasy and start thrashing about for more activity. Then when we have managed to remove the outer distractions, the inner ones start up—doubts, fears, conflicts, unsettled feelings and desires. So we go back and encounter the outer noise again. We can find all kinds of reasons for not being alone, but in time we will cherish this time alone with God as more and more as we enjoy communion with Him.

~CLARA M. MATHESON (contemporary)
Journal

We need not wings to go in search of Him,
but have only to find a place where we can be alone—and
look upon Him present within us.

~TERESA OF AVILA (1515-1582)

It is important that we get still to wait on God. And it is best that we get alone, preferably with our Bible outspread before us. Then if we will we may draw near to God and begin to hear Him speak to us in our hearts. I think for the average person the progression will be something like this: First a sound as of a Presence walking in the garden. Then a voice, more intelligible, but still far from clear. Then the happy moment when the Spirit begins to illuminate the Scriptures, and that which had been only a sound at best, now becomes an intelligible word, warm and intimate and clear as the word of a dear friend. Then will come life and light, and best of all, ability to see and rest in and embrace Jesus Christ as Savior and Lord of all.

~A. W. TOZER (1897-1963)
The Pursuit of God

Let us be silent that we may hear the whisper of God.
~RALPH WALDO EMERSON (1803-1882)

Lord, the Scripture says: "There is a time for silence and a time for speech." Saviour, teach me the silence of humility, the silence of wisdom, the silence of faith. Lord, teach me to silence my own heart that I may listen to the gentle movement of the Holy Spirit within me and sense the depths which are of God.

~FRANKFURT PRAYER (LATE 1500'S)

Mary was not praised for sitting still; but for
her sitting at Jesus' feet.
~CHARLES H. SPURGEON (1834-1892)
Morning and Evening Devotions

Martha was too busy doing things for Jesus to be still and be with Him. She was more occupied with her cause than with Christ. Mary, however, savored the opportunity to be with God. Martha viewed the evening as dinner for God. Mary viewed the evening as dinner with God.

~Eric Geiger (contemporary):
Identity: Who You Are in Christ

How can you expect God to speak in that gentle and inward voice which melts the soul, when you are making so much noise? Be silent and God will speak again.

~François de Fénelon (1651-1717)
Spiritual Maxims

Communion with God was never more needful than now. Feverish activity rules in all spheres of life...We are so busy thinking, discussing, defending, inquiring, or preaching and teaching and working, that we have no time, and no leisure of heart for quiet contemplation, without which the exercise of the intellect upon Christ's truth will not feed, and busy activity in Christ's cause may starve the soul.

~Alexander Maclaren
(1828-1910)

How rare it is to find a soul quiet enough to hear God speak.

~François de Fénelon (1651-1717)
Instructions

In this noisy, restless, bewildering age, there is a great need for quietness of spirit. Even in our communion with God we are so busy presenting our problems, asking for help, seeking relief that we leave no moments of silence to listen for God's answers. By practice we can learn to submerge our spirits beneath the turbulent surface waves of life and reach that depth of our being where all is still, where no storms can reach us.

~ALICE HEGAN RICE (1870-1942)
My Pillow Book

The very best and utmost of attainment in this life is to remain still and let God act and speak in thee.

~MEISTER ECKHART (c.1260-1327)
Meister Eckhart Speaks

There is a connection between God and stillness. There is a sense in which God never seems so near to me as when everything about me is hushed and I myself am quiet and still. I do not say He is any nearer then than when I am pressed by many duties, but it is in those moments I myself am most conscious of His presence.

~HARRY BISSEKER (20th cent.)

Silence is a gift of God,
to let us speak more intimately with God.

~VINCENT PALLOTTI (1600?-1661)

The Essence Of Serenity Is Within

The best and most beautiful things in the world
cannot be seen or even touched. They must be felt with the heart.

~HELEN KELLER (1880-1968)
The Story of My Life

Glorious indeed is the world of God
around us, but more glorious the world of God within us.
~HENRY WADSWORTH LONGFELLOW (1807-1882)
Hyperion

The continual mistake is that we do not concentrate upon the present day, the actual hour, of our life: we live in the past or in the future: we are continually expecting the coming of some special hour when our life shall unfold itself in its full significance.

~ALEXANDER YELCHANINOV (1881-1934)
Fragments of a Diary

We keep running because we falsely think that fulfillment is always there, not here. We love noise and excitement because we have nothing inside. It distracts us and makes us forget our loneliness and helps us escape from ourselves.

~CLARA M. MATHESON (contemporary)
Journal

Rushing is a sign of weakness.
Quiet abiding is a sign of strength.
~A. J. RUSSELL (1867-1935):
God at Eventide

If we fill our lives with things, and again with things; if we consider ourselves so unimportant that we must fill every moment of our lives with action, when will we have the time to make the long, slow journey across the desert as did the magi? Or sit and watch the stars as did the shepherds? Or brood over the coming of the child as did Mary?

~AUTHOR UNKNOWN

Serenity comes not alone by removing
the outward causes and occasions of fear, but
by the discovery of inward reservoirs to draw upon.

~RUFUS M. JONES (1863-1948)
The Testimony of the Soul

Among the common people whom we know, it is not necessarily those who are busiest, not those who, meteor-like, are ever on the rush after some visible charge and work. It is the lives, like the stars, which simply pour down on us the calm light of their bright and faithful being, up to which we look and out of which we gather the deepest calm and courage.

~PHILLIPS BROOKS (1835-1893)
Sermons

The reason we are not fully at ease in heart and soul
is because we seek rest in these things that are so little and
have no rest within them, and pay no attention
to our God, who is the only real rest.

~JULIAN OF NORWICH (c.1342-1413)

For the many wants which disturb life, which make us uneasy to ourselves, quarrelsome with others, and unthankful to God; which weary us in vain labors and foolish anxieties; which carry us from project to project, and from place to place in a poor pursuit of we know not what, are the wants which neither God, nor nature, nor reason hath subjected us to, but are solely infused into us by pride, envy, ambition, and covetousness.

~WILLIAM LAW (1686-1761)
A Serious Call to a Devout and Holy Life

I will not hurry through this day!
Lord, I will listen by the way,
To humming bees and singing birds,
To speaking trees and friendly words;
And for the moments in between
Seek glimpses of Thy great Unseen.
I will not hurry through this day;
I will take time to think and pray;
I will look up into the sky,
Where fleecy clouds and swallows fly;
And somewhere in the day, maybe
I will catch a whisper, Lord, from Thee!

~Ralph S. Cushman (1879-1960)
Hilltop Verses and Prayers

Closing Prayer

Lord, teach me to listen. The times are noisy and my ears are weary with the thousand harsh sounds which continuously assault them. Let me hear You speaking in my heart. Let me get used to the sound of Your voice when the sounds of earth die away and the only sound will be the music of Your voice.
Amen.

Chapter 11

Cultivating Humility

The Flowers Bloom Where They are Planted

Humility is a strange flower; it grows best in winter weather, and under storms of affliction.
~Samuel Rutherford (1600?-1661)

The absolute gift is the gift of oneself, such as Jesus practiced. By forgetting ourselves, we find ourselves, and are able to draw near to God. If we truly feel that by ourselves we are nothing—then there is room for God to come in and be everything. In exercising personal rights we are building up animosity and ill will. When we serve humbly, then what can disturb the serenity of the soul? A person can learn nothing at all until he first learns humility. It is a sure sign of strength and contentment. Humility removes every hindrance to faith. In the Roman centurion's humbling himself before Jesus, Jesus said, "I have not found anyone in Israel with such great faith" *(Luke 7:9).*

Pride Leads To Spiritual Blindness

When pride comes, then comes disgrace,
but with humility comes wisdom.
~PROVERBS 11:2

Pride is essentially competitive. Pride gets no pleasure out of having something, only out of having more of it than the next man. We say that people are proud of being rich, or clever, or good-looking, but they are not. They are proud of being richer, or cleverer, or better-looking than others. If every one else became equally rich, or clever, or good-looking there would be nothing to be proud about. It is the comparison that makes you proud: the pleasure of being above the rest. Once the element of competition has gone, pride has gone….As long as you are proud you cannot know God. A proud man is always looking down on things and people: and, of course, as long as you are looking down, you cannot see something that is above you.

~C. S. LEWIS (1898-1963):
Mere Christianity

The proud man is deaf and blind to the world;
he does not see the world, but only himself reflected in all things.
~ALEXANDER YELCHANINOV (1881-1934)
Fragments of a Diary

Do not expose others' weaknesses in order to make them feel less able than you. Neither should you think on your superior skill with any delight, or use it to set yourself above another person. Remember that what is most important to God is that we submit ourselves and all that we have to him.

~JEREMY TAYLOR (1613-1667)
The Rule and Exercises of Holy Living

Patience with ourselves is a duty for Christians
and the only real humility. For it means patience with a
growing creature whom God has taken in hand and
whose completion he will effect in his own time and way.

~EVELYN UNDERHILL (1857-1941)

It is better to have but little knowledge with humility and understanding, than great learning which might make you proud. For a man's merits are not to be estimated by his having many visions, or by his knowledge of the Bible, or by his being placed in a higher position; but by his being grounded in true humility, and by his seeking always, purely, and entirely, the honor of God.

~THOMAS À KEMPIS (1380-1471)
The Imitation of Christ

Very often the way in which a thing is done says
more than a thousand words. Humility is not merely an attitude;
it manifests itself also in the quality of the deed.

~HOWARD THURMAN (1900-1981)
The Inward Journey

Pride ultimately leads to spiritual blindness. When we make ourselves the center of all our activities and thought we become hardened to the feelings and desires of others. We think we see clearly, but in reality, this pride causes us to become blind to the needs of those around us and to God's plan for our lives. We do not see our own weakness.

~CLARA M. MATHESON (contemporary)
Journal

Whoever exalts himself will be humbled,
and whoever humbles himself will be exalted.
~MATTHEW 23:12

The pride of the good man is one of the deadliest sins of all, and for that reason in the parable of the prodigal son the virtuous brother who stayed at home was all the time farther away from the father's house than the younger son returning from the far country with nothing but a broken and contrite heart.

~T. M. TAYLOR (20th cent.)
University of Edinburg Journal, no. 2

God Gives Grace To The Humble

Welcome with open arms fellow
believers who don't see things the way you do.
~ROMANS 14:1 (MSG)

As long as we are full of self we are shocked
at the faults of others. Let us think often of our own sin,
and we shall be lenient of the sins of others.
~FRANÇOIS DE FÉNELON (1651-1717)
Instructions

There are plenty to follow our Lord half-way, but not the other half. They will give up possessions, friends and honors, but it touches them too closely to disown themselves.

~MEISTER ECKHART (c.1260-1327
Meister Eckhart Speaks

Do nothing out of selfish ambition or vain conceit, but in humility consider others better than yourselves. Each of you should look not only to your own interests, but also to the interests of others.

~PHILIPPIANS 2:3-4

Do you desire to be great? Make yourself little. There is a mysterious connection between real advancement and self-abasement. If you minister to the humble and despised, if you feed the hungry, tend the sick, succor the distressed; if you bear with the forward, submit to insult, endure ingratitude, render good for evil, you are, as by a divine charm, getting power over the world and rising among the creatures. God has established this law. Thus He does His wonderful works.

~JOHN HENRY NEWMAN (1801-1890)
Parochial and Plain Sermons

If you want to be miserable, think much about yourself; about what you want, what you like, what respect people ought to pay you, and what people think of you.

~CHARLES KINGSLEY (1819-1875)
Sermons for the Times

The secret of knowing God's complete sufficiency is in coming to the end of everything in ourselves and our circumstances. Once we reach this point...we will then turn from our circumstances to God, realizing they are the evidence of Him working in our lives.

~ALBERT B. SIMPSON (1844-1919)
The Life of A.B. Simpson

Whoever wants to become great among you must first be your servant, just as the Son of Man did not come to be served, but to serve, and to give his life as a ransom for many.

~MATTHEW 20:27-28

As long as our mind is stayed on our dear selves, we will never have peace. Some people think more of themselves than of all the rest of the world. It is self in the morning, self at noon, and self at night. It is self when they wake up, and self when they go to bed. They are all the time looking at themselves and thinking about themselves instead of "looking unto Jesus." Faith does not look within; it looks without. It is not what I think, or what I feel, or what I have done, but it is what Jesus Christ is and has done, that is the important thing for us to dwell upon.

~DWIGHT L. MOODY (1837-1899), in
A Treasury of Sermons Illustrations

All of you clothe yourselves with humility
toward one another because God opposes the proud,
but gives grace to the humble.
~I PETER 5:5

Denying Self Leads To Peace

God walks with the humble; he reveals himself to the lowly; he gives understanding to the little ones; he discloses his meaning to pure minds, but hides his grace from the curious and the proud.

~THOMAS À KEMPIS (1380-1471)
The Imitation of Christ

Humble yourselves before the Lord
and He will lift you up.
~JAMES 4:10

It is no great thing to be humble
when you are brought low; but to be humble
when you are praised is a great and rare attainment.
~BERNARD OF CLAIRVAUX (1090-1153)
Letters

I am sure that you understand that it is not enough to be merely separated from the world. For we can be separated and be quite proud about it....You cannot imagine how dangerous pride is, especially if it is that pride of wisdom and morality which seems so right and kind.
~FRANÇOIS DE FÉNELON (1651-1717)
Spiritual Letters

Humility is not weakness but strength, for it receives the strength of God. It is not folly, but wisdom, for it is open to every available wisdom of God. It is not nothingness but fullness, for into the vacuum created by the demolition of human pride and self-sufficiency, pours the fullness of God.
~ALBERT E. DAY (1884-1973)
Discipline and Discovery

Lord, grant that I may seek rather
to comfort than to be comforted;
to understand than to be understood;
to love than to be loved;
For it is by forgetting self that one finds;
it is by forgiving that one is forgiven;
it is by dying that one awakes to eternal life.
~TERESA OF AVILA (1515-1582)

Should you ask me what are the ways of God, I would tell you that the first is humility; the second is humility; and the third is still humility. Not that there are no other precepts to give, but if humility does not precede all that we do, our efforts are fruitless.

~St. Augustine (354-430)

Humility is man's path to God,
mercy the path on which God comes to meet humanity.

~Meister Eckhart (c.1260-1327)
Meister Eckhart Speaks

How arrogant of us to put ourselves at the center when only He belongs there. If we try to force our ideas upon others, we tend to become loud and demanding, and cannot tolerate someone else having the last word. If we are always seeing the bad in a situation, we become prone to becoming argumentative and bitter, and tend to kill the spirit of joyfulness which signifies union with God.

~Isabelle Baker (contemporary)
Unpublished Writings

It is not humility to insist on being someone
that you are not. It is as much as saying that you
know better than God who you are and who you ought to be.
How do you expect to arrive at the end of your own journey
if you take the road to another man's city?

~Thomas Merton (1915-1968)
Seeds of Contemplation

Be completely humble and gentle;
be patience, bearing with one another in love.

~Ephesians 4:2

Jesus—Our Example Of Humility

If anyone would come after me, he must deny himself and take up his cross and follow me.
~MATTHEW 16:24

"He that loseth his life for my sake shall find it" *(Matthew 10:39)*. This paradox from the lips of Jesus is ultimate wisdom.
~ALBERT E. DAY (1884-1973)
Discipline and Discovery

It is Jesus who gives us this lesson of meekness and humility; no other being could have taught it without our revolting at it....We have only to be silent and adore, to admire and to imitate. The Son of God has descended upon the earth, and taken upon himself a mortal body, and expired upon the cross, that he might teach us humility. Who shall not be humble now?….Humility is the source of all true greatness: pride is ever impatience, ready to be offended. He who thinks nothing is due to him, never thinks himself ill-treated.
~FRANÇOIS DE FÉNELON (1651-1717)
"On Meekness and Humility"

Take my yoke upon you and learn from me, for I am gentle and humble in heart, and you will find rest for your souls.
~MATTHEW 11:29

The teachings of Jesus are profound. The way to inner power lies in the realization of helplessness. The way to independence lies through dependence on God, and the way to true freedom lies in surrendering to God, the way to find self is to give up self. In Jesus' life of service, he rejected the traditional concept of power and position. He treated women with respect and insisted upon washing his disciples' feet. His whole life was a testimony of service and submission.
CLARA M. MATHESON (contemporary)
Journal

Christ tells us that if we want to join him, we shall travel
the way he took. It is surely not right that the Son of God should
go his way on the path of shame while
the sons of men walk the way of worldly honor.

~JOHN OF THE CROSS (1542-1591)
The Complete Works of John of the Cross

*Don't be selfish; don't live to make a good
impression on others. Be humble, thinking of others as
better than yourself. Don't just think about your own affairs,
but be interested in others, too... Your attitude
should be the kind that was shown us by Jesus Christ,
who though he was God, did not demand and cling to his rights
as God, but laid aside his mighty power
and glory taking the disguise of a slave and becoming like men.*

~PHILIPPIANS 2:3-7 (TLB)

The principle runs through all life from top to bottom. Give up yourself, and you will find your real self. Lose your life and you will save it. Submit to death, death of your ambitions and favorite wishes everyday and death of your whole body in the end: submit with every fiber of your being, and you will find eternal life. Keep back nothing. Nothing that you have not given away will ever be really yours. Nothing in you that has not died will ever be raised from the dead. Look for yourself, and you will find in the long run only hatred, loneliness, despair, rage, ruin, and decay. But look for Christ and you will find Him, and with Him everything else thrown in.

~C. S. LEWIS (1898-1963)
Mere Christianity

God's Definition Of Success

We often confuse outward success with inward success—the more distinctions and honors we receive, the more we are valued. This is not Jesus' way. He was despised, spat upon, stoned and jeered at by the mob. We are not doing the work of the world. Why do we expect its pay?

~CATHERINE DE RAMBOUILLET (20th cent.)
Ramblings

It is not good to eat too much honey,
nor is it honorable to seek one's own honor.
~PROVERBS 25:27

You know how difficult it is amidst the
honors, riches and influences of the world to lend an ear to God.
~JOHN CALVIN (1509-1564), in a letter to an invalid

Merit, whether it be esteem, respect, honor or distinction is a human appraisal. No man standing in the Hall of Final Judgment will venture to say, "I was honored of men, I received praise and distinction..." He will be happy if he can say, "I did my best where I was: I finished the work you gave me to do."

~RAYNOR C. JOHNSON (1901-1987)
The Imprisoned Splendour

Should you then seek great things for
yourself? Seek them not.
~JEREMIAH 45:5

Great tranquility has he who cares for neither praise nor blame. You are not a better person because you are praised, not the worse for being blamed. Man looks at the face, but God looks into the heart. Man considers the actions, but God weighs the intentions.

~THOMAS À KEMPIS (1380-1471)
The Imitation of Christ

Whatever you may possess, and however fruitful your activities, regard them all as worthless without the inward certainty and experience of Jesus' love.

~AUTHOR UNKNOWN (14th cent.)
The Cloud of Unknowing

He who can find pearls will not stop to pick up shells, and so a man who aims at real goodness will not be keen about outward tokens of honor.

~FRANCIS DE SALES (1567-1622)
Introduction to the Devout Life

A humble man can do great things with an uncommon perfection because he is no longer concerned about incidentals, like his own interests and his own reputation, and therefore he no longer needs to waste his efforts in defending them....Humility is the surest sign of strength.

~THOMAS MERTON (1915-1963)
New Seeds of Contemplation

Lord, make me childlike. Deliver me from the urge to compete with another for a place or prestige or position...Deliver me from pose and pretense. Help me to forget myself and find true peace in beholding Thee. Amen

~A. W. TOZER (1897-1963)
The Pursuit of God

Do you see a man wise in his own eyes?
There is more hope for a fool than for him.
~PROVERBS 26:12

The "poor in spirit" are happy because they do not make demands on others and complain about their circumstances. They do not insist on their own rights, and they do not look to what good they are going to get. They are strong enough to be considered total failures in the eyes of the world. While serving and ministering to others they wish to be unseen. They never use people for their own advantage, never talk of themselves and never desire to be first.

~CLARA M. MATHESON (contemporary)
Journal

The man who thinks he knows something does not
yet know what he ought to know.
~I CORINTHIANS 8:2

Closing Prayer

O Lord, what do we expect to reap if we
seek to appear great in the eyes of men? What does it
matter whether we are ridiculed and regarded as insignificant
by men, if in Your eyes we are great and
without fault? Oh, will we ever understand this truth?
~BERNARD OF CLAIRVAUX (1090-1153)

Chapter 12

Welcoming Simplicity

The Fruit Provides Nourishment for the Gardener

A hard, materialized heart, like a wayside soul gives God no access. A heart that is shallow, like thin soil on stony ground, gives a quick response, but offers no sustenance to God's truth and therefore no harvest. A heart absorbed in many mundane concerns, like thorny ground, soon chokes the spiritual aspirations to death. Only the heart that is clean, simple, and cultivated, like a plowed weeded field, can receive and nurture the truth of God and reap a harvest of godly character.

~Albert E. Day (1884-1973)
Discipline and Discovery

As our lives become more God-filled, our tastes become simpler, and our lives become marked by simplicity. We need fewer acquaintances, but more friends, fewer duties, but more faithful service, fewer books, but better ones. Doing away with the superfluous will help us attain a singleness of purpose. We recognize that what one is has nothing to do with what one possesses. Conformity to other's ideas means little to us, for our greatest duty lies in pleasing God by finding and doing what He has called us to do.

Our Example Of Simplicity Is Jesus

*As servants of God we commend ourselves
in every way: poor, yet making many rich;...having nothing,
and yet possessing everything.*
~II CORINTHIANS 6:4,10

Don't confuse your meals with your life, and your clothes with your body. Don't lose your head over what perishes. Nearly everything does perish: so face the facts, don't rush after the transient and unreal. Maintain your soul in tranquil dependence on God; don't mistake what you possess for what you are. Accumulating things is useless… The simpler your house, the easier it will be to run. The fewer the things and the people you simply must have, the nearer you will be to the ideal of happiness—as having nothing, to possess all.
~EVELYN UNDERHILL (1857-1941)
The House of the Soul

Possessiveness is, by its intrinsic nature, insatiable. The man with a million dollars, far from being satisfied, wants more. The solution to this problem will come, if it comes at all, not by acquiring more, but by finding an inner peace which renders the hectic pace unnecessary.
~D. ELTON TRUEBLOOD (1900-1994):
A New Man for Our Time

The wise man carries his possessions within him.
~BIAS OF PRIENE (6th cent B.C.)

The simplicity which is in Christ is rarely found among us. In its stead are programs, methods, organizations and a world of nervous activities which occupy time and attention but can never satisfy the longing of the heart.

~A. W. TOZER (1897-1963)
The Pursuit of God

Then Jesus said to them, "Beware! Don't always be wishing for what you don't have. For real life and real living are not related to how rich we are.

~LUKE 12:15 (TLB)

Wisdom leads us back to childhood. "Except we become as little children we shall not enter the Kingdom of Heaven"

~BLAISE PASCAL (1623-1662)
Pensées (Thoughts)

We must hold our treasures as if we did not hold them; possess them, but not let them possess us; lay them at Christ's feet and serve Him through them.

~ALEXANDER YELCHANINOV (1881-1934)
Fragments of a Diary

When one begins to practice simplicity, the ego is deprived of the very strategy by which it sustains itself. Nothing will deflate the ego more effectively than to be recognized for what it is. It lives by pretension. It dies when the mask is torn away and the stark reality is exposed to the gaze of others. Simplicity also avails in braking the tyranny of things. Ostentation, artificiality, ornamentation, pretentious style, luxury—all require things… What one is does not depend upon what one has.

~ALBERT E. DAY (1884-1973)
Discipline and Discovery

*Any one of you who does not give up everything
he has cannot by my disciple.*
~LUKE 14:33

Jesus Christ was simplicity itself; always the same, without any affectation in His speech or actions. He taught, with the authority of God made Man, the most sublime truths, and things which had before been unknown. But He propounded His doctrine in a simple, familiar manner, without any pomp or human eloquence, and so that all minds could understand Him. His miracles divine in themselves, are still more divine from the way in which He performed them.

~JEAN-NICOLAS GROU (1731-1803)
Manual for Interior Souls

To have what we want
is riches, but to be able to do without is power.
~GEORGE MACDONALD (1824-1905)
Unspoken Sermons

When we are surrendered to God, we are not grasping for pleasure, and even our troubles are received with thanksgiving. This inner harmony, and this deliverance from fear and the tormenting desires of self, create a satisfaction in the soul which is above all the intoxicating joys of this world put together.

~FRANÇOIS DE FÉNELON (1651-1717)
Spiritual Letters

We cannot, by observing rules, make ourselves simple. All we can do is to show our desire to remove the hindrances in our Lord's way, to empty ourselves so that we may be filled with the simplicity which is in Christ Jesus.

~BEDE FROST (early 20th cent.)

In this world it is not what we take up,
but what we give up, that makes us rich.
~HENRY WARD BEECHER (1813-1887)
Life Thoughts

God has given you a simplicity and candor which doubtless pleases him very much. It is on this foundation that he wants to build. He wants from you a simplicity which will be as much his wisdom as it is not your own. He wants you to be small in your own eyes, and yielding in his hands like a little child. It is this childlikeness, so contrary to the spirit of man, and so urged in the Gospel, which God wants to put in your heart despite the corruption which rules in the world. It is by his simplicity and this littleness that he wants to heal you of whatever remains of lofty and cynical wisdom.
~FRANÇOIS DE FÉNELON (1651-1717)
Spiritual Letters

Trust in your money and down you go.
Trust in God and flourish as a tree.
~PROVERBS 11:28 (TLB)

Man hungers for more than the world can give. He "cannot live by bread alone." When we realize that, when we realize that we have much to live for, we do not seem to need so much to live on.
~RALPH W. SOCKMAN (1889-1970)
The Higher Happiness

Finding Freedom In Simplicity

So if the Son sets you free, you will be free indeed.
~JOHN 8:36

There can be no doubt that this possessive clinging to things is one of the most harmful habits in life. Because it is so natural, it is rarely recognized for the evil it is.

~A. W. TOZER (1897-1963)
The Pursuit of God

Do not store up for yourselves treasures on earth, where moth and rust destroy, and where thieves break in and steal.

~MATTHEW 6:19-21

Only the simple are the free. All the rest are under the tyranny of the ambitious ego, its demand for recognition and for things, and the preoccupation with people. Hence, only the simple are free to direct their attention to God steadily, uninterruptedly, and to enter into conscious, vivid, and redemptive fellowship with God. No wonder Jesus said, "Except ye be converted, and become as little children, ye shall not enter into the kingdom of heaven" *(Matthew 18:2).*

~ALBERT E. DAY (1884-1973)
Discipline and Discovery

A Christian man is the most free lord of all,
and subject to none; a Christian man is the most dutiful
servant of all, and subject to everyone.

~MARTIN LUTHER (1483-1546)
Table Talk of Martin Luther

Closing Prayer

Strengthen me in my inner self, O God, by the
grace of your Holy Spirit; May I put away from my heart
all useless anxiety and distress, and let me never be drawn aside
by various longings after anything whatever, but may I regard
all possessions as passing away. Amen.

Part Five

The Developing Soul

Keeping the Garden in Tip-Top Condition

What an inexpressible comfort it is to know that my Father is the gardener. Pruning seems to be destroying the vine, and the gardener appears to be cutting everything away. Yet he sees the future and knows that the final result will be the enrichment of the life of the vine, and a greater abundance of fruit.

~JAMES R. MILLER (1640-1912)
Glimpses through Life's Windows

Chapter 13

Persisting Faithfully

Pruning and Weeding Involve Periods of Distress

We want to labor in the fields, water, and till, aware that it is God who causes the plants to grow. The harvest is totally God's business and he doesn't need us to keep score on Him.

~Charles W. Colson (contemporary)
Life Sentence

Faithfulness in important and conspicuous things is common, but faithfulness in the little ordinary things is what shows real love. Great spiritual profit comes from doing little unconscious deeds of kindness which are not sought, loving those who think ill of us and giving to those who cannot give in return. All faith involves discipline. True discipline requires the application in all areas of our lives of the principle laid out in God's Word. Often we are willing to embark upon some great adventure or do anything, but wait patiently upon the Lord. We must be like those who stumble and fall while running a race, yet rise and press on to the goal, not looking back.

We Are Called To Be Faithful

I don't claim anything of the work. It is his work. I am like a little pencil in his hand. That is all. He does the thinking. He does the writing. The pencil has nothing to do with it. The pencil has only to be allowed to be used.

~MOTHER TERESA OF CALCUTTA (1910-1997)
Speech, Awakening Conference, June 15, 1986

Whatever you do, work at it with all your heart,
as working for the Lord, not for man.
~COLOSSIANS 3:23

The mark of a saint is not perfection, but
consecration. A saint is not a man without faults, but a man
who has given himself without reserve to God.
~BROOKE FOSS WESTCOTT (1825-1901)
Lectures

Perseverance must finish its work so that
you may be mature and complete, not lacking anything.
~JAMES 1:4

It is well to remember that even in the holiest undertaking, what God requires of us is earnest willing labor, and the use of such means as we can command; but He does not require success of us: that depends solely upon Himself, and sometimes in His very love for us He refuses to crown our best intentions with success.

~JEAN-NICOLAS GROU (1731-1803)
Manual for Interior Souls

Through all our difficulties of circumstance, health, opportunity and even of temperamental personalities that we come daily into contact with, God reaches us and guides us to the destination He has planned for us. The events by which he shapes and disciplines us are often difficult, but our humble acceptance of everything ensures us of deeper communion with Him. Let us be faithful to the calling.

~CLARA M. MATHESON (contemporary)
Journal

O Lord, we put our hope and trust in You.
Renew our strength. Help us to soar on wings
like eagles; to run and not grow weary,
to walk and not be faint.

~ISAIAH 40:31

Nothing is small or great in God's sight; whatever He wills becomes great to us, however seemingly trifling. Once the voice of the Spirit tells us that He requires anything of us we have no right to measure its importance. On the other hand, whatever He would not have us do, however important we may think it, is as nothing to us. How do you know what you may lose by neglecting this duty, which you think is trifling, or the blessing which its faithful performance may bring? Give yourself to Him, trust Him, fix your eye upon Him, listen to His voice, and then go on bravely and cheerfully.

~JEAN-NICOLAS GROU (1731-1803)
Manual for Interior Souls

The best preparation for tomorrow is to
do today's work superbly well.

~WILLIAM OSLER (1849-1919)

God Causes The Plants To Grow, But We Are To Be Faithful To Their Care

The beginner must think of himself as of one setting out to make a garden in which the Lord is to take His delight, yet in soil most unfruitful and full of weeds. His Majesty uproots the weeds and will set good plants in their stead.... We have now, by God's help, like good gardeners, to make these plants grow, and to water them carefully, so that they may not perish, but may produce flowers.

~TERESA OF AVILA (1515-1582)
Interior Castle

"He who is faithful over a few things is a lord of cities." It does not matter whether you preach in Westminster Abbey, or teach a ragged class, so you be faithful. The faithfulness is all.

~GEORGE MACDONALD (1824-1905)
Unspoken Sermons

Nothing comes by pure accident, not even the interruptions in our busy day. And such as follow on to know God's will see in all events what may lead to good, and so trust grows into a habit, as habit grows by perpetual use, till every circumstance may be seen to be but a fresh manifestation of the will of God working itself out in us.

~THOMAS T. CARTER (19th cent.)

Let love and faithfulness never leave you;
bind them around your neck,
write them on the tablet of your heart.

~PROVERBS 3:3

It is the habit of making sacrifices in small things that enables us for making them in great, when it is asked of us. Temper, love of preeminence, bodily indulgence, the quick retort, the sharp irony. In checking these let us find our cross and carry it. Or, when the moment comes for some really great service, the heart will be petrified for it, and the blinded eyes will not see the occasion of love.

~ANTHONY W. THOROLD (1825-1894)

Be faithful, even to the point of death,
and I will give you the crown of life.

~REVELATION 2:10

Have courage for the great sorrows of life and patience for the small ones; and when you have laboriously accomplished your daily tasks, go to sleep in peace. God is awake.

~VICTOR HUGO (1802-1885)

Great works do not always lie in our way, but every moment we may do little ones excellently, that is, with great love. Our Lord Himself has told us that "He that is faithful in that which is least is faithful also in much."

~FRANCIS DE SALES (1567-1622)
Introduction to the Devout Life

There are years in South Africa when locusts swarm the land and eat the crops. They come in hordes, blocking out the sun. The crops are lost and a hard winter follows. The "years that the locusts eat" are feared and dreaded. But the year after the locusts, South Africa reaps its greatest crops, for the dead bodies of the locusts serve as fertilizer for the new seed. And the locust year is restored as great crops swell the land.

This is a parable of our life. There are seasons of deep distress and afflictions that sometimes eat all the usefulness of our lives away. Yet, the promise is that God will restore those locust years if we endure. We will reap if we faint not. Although now we do not know all the 'why's,' we can be assured our times are in His hands.

~RON HEMBREE (contemporary)
Fruits of the Spirit

See how the farmer waits for the land to yield its valuable crop and how patient he is for autumn and spring rains. You too, be patient and stand firm.
~JAMES 5:7-8

The Development Of Christ-Like Character

There is no more searching test of the human spirit than the way it behaves when fortune is adverse and it has to pass through a prolonged period of disappointing failures. Then comes the real proof of the man. Achievement, if a man has the ability, is a joy; but to take hard knocks and come up smiling, to have your mainsail blown away and then rig a sheet on the bowsprit and sail on—this is perhaps the deepest test of character.

~HARRY EMERSON FOSDICK (1878-1969)
On Being a Real Person

A man may be outwardly successful all his life long, and die hollow and worthless as a puff-ball; and he may be externally defeated all his life long, and die in the royalty of a kingdom established within him. A man's true estate of power and riches is to be in God, not in his dwelling, or position, or external relations.

~HENRY WARD BEECHER (1831-1887)
Life Thoughts

Character cannot be developed in ease and quiet.
Only through experience of trial and
suffering can the soul be strengthened, vision cleared,
ambition inspired, and success achieved.

~HELEN KELLER (1880-1968)
The Story of My Life

The tests of life are to make, not break us. Trouble may demolish a man's business but build up his character. The blow at the outward man may be the greatest blessing to the inner man. If God then puts or permits anything hard in our lives, be sure that the real peril, the real trouble, is that we shall lose if we flinch or rebel.

~MALTBIE D. BABCOCK (1858-1901)
Thoughts for Every-Day Living

What good will it be for a man if he gains the
whole world, yet forfeits his soul.

~MATTHEW 16:26

Character is the product of daily, hourly actions, words and thoughts: daily forgiveness, unselfishness, kindnesses, sympathies, charities, sacrifices for the good of others, struggles against temptation, submissiveness under trial. It is these, like the blinding colors in a picture, or the blending notes of music, which constitute the man.

~JOHN MACDUFF (1818-1895)
Letters and Articles

The man of integrity walks securely,
but he who takes crooked paths will be found out.
~PROVERBS 10:9

Goodness cannot be measured in any way.
It is impossible to say who has done more good and who less.
Doesn't it all depend upon one's motives? Some do good because
of the love in their heart and some do good for
show, their motive cleverly camouflaged.
~CLARA M. MATHESON (contemporary)
Journal

If we claim to have fellowship with him yet walk in the
darkness, we lie and do not live by the truth.
~I JOHN 1:6

Some folk think they may scold, rail, hate,
rob, and kill too, so it be but for God's sake. But
nothing in us unlike Him can please Him.
~WILLIAM PENN (1644-1718)
Some Fruits of Solitude

Our lack of compassion, our ruthlessness towards other men, is an impenetrable curtain between ourselves and God. It is as if we had covered a plant with a black hood, and then complained that it died from deprivation of sunlight.

~ALEXANDER YELCHANINOV (1881-1934)
Fragments of a Diary

A man of integrity is a true man, a bold man, and a steady man; he is to be trusted and relied upon. No bribes can corrupt him, no fear daunt him; his word is slow in coming, but sure. He shines brightest in the fire, and his friend hears of him most when he most needs him. His courage grows with danger, and conquers opposition by constancy…He runs with truth, and not with the times; with right and not with might.

~WILLIAM PENN (1644-1718)
"Advice to His Children"

Closing Prayer

Lord, purify my motives that I might
always do all things with the intention of pleasing You.
Help me never to knowingly speak anything
that is not strictly true, and to always
remember that You are the
Source of Truth. In Jesus' name.
Amen.

Chapter 14

Recognizing The Value Of Times Of Struggle

Strong Winds Cause the Plant to Be Strengthened

How many earthly desires and worldly feelings are shaken from the soul by the tempest of a great sorrow, even as the faded leaves of autumn. But when all the leaves are stripped from the tree, and it stands bare and desolate under the lashings of winter winds, there still remain, carefully sealed up on every branch and twig, buds of celestial hue, which are to unfold in leaf and flower in the summer of God's kingdom.

~Harriet Beecher Stowe (1811-1896)

Occasional night and shadows are better for flowers than continual sun. Adversity tests a plant's vigor and toughness. We are like flowers. Discouragement, adversity and trials come. Suffering is a necessary part of life so that we may learn to adapt our lives to the teaching God has given us, realize our own weakness, and develop obedience, perseverance and fortitude. Times of suffering will soften our hearts and strengthen our faith. As a butterfly struggles to escape its cocoon and in so doing becomes strong enough to fly, so God allows difficulties in our lives so we may develop enough strength to fly with spiritual wings.

God Touches Our Lives Through Suffering

No Christian escapes a taste of the
wilderness on the way to the Promised Land.
~EVELYN UNDERHILL (1857-1941)
The Fruits of the Spirit

The marvelous richness of human experience would lose something of rewarding joy if there were no limitations to overcome. The hilltop hour would not be half so wonderful if there were no dark valleys to traverse.

~HELEN KELLER (1880-1968)
The Story of My Life

I willingly bear witness to the fact that I
owe more to my Lord's fire, hammer, and the file
than to anything else in His workshop.
~CHARLES H. SPURGEON (1834-1892)
Morning and Evening Devotions

God whispers to us in our pleasure, speaks
in our conscience, but shouts in our pain: it is His
megaphone to rouse a deaf world.
~C. S. LEWIS (1898-1963)
The Problem of Pain

The Good Shepherd suffered. Why should we be lambs who are petted and protected. The practice of positive thinking—now better known as possibility thinking—or even by nights of fervent prayer, cannot permanently prevent the river from rising. Neither should we expect that when the river rises God will whisk us out of the flood with his heavenly helicopter. We ought to anticipate trouble, but not be shaken by it.

~VERNON GROUNDS (contemporary), in
Charles W. Colson's *Life Sentence*

Because of my chains, most of the brothers in the Lord have been encouraged to speak the word of God more courageously and fearlessly.

~PHILIPPIANS 1:14

No flowers wear so lovely a blue as those which grow at the foot of the frozen glacier; no stars gleam so brightly as those which glisten in the polar sky; no water tastes so sweet as that which springs amid the desert sand; and no faith is so precious as that which lives and triumphs in adversity. Tried faith brings experience. You could not have believed your own weakness had you not been compelled to pass through the rivers; and you would never have known God's strength had you not been supported amid the water-floods.

~CHARLES H. SPURGEON (1834-1892)
Morning and Evening Devotions

Every flower, even the most beautiful, has its own shadow beneath it as it basks in the sunlight.

~L. B. COWMAN (20th cent.)
Streams in the Desert

When early American apple growers had trouble with their apple trees growing too fast while producing little fruit, they corrected the problem with a deep gash to the tree trunk. Instead of growing into a big, woody plant, it converted its energy into an abundance of apples. We are often like unpruned apple trees that misdirect their energies into unproductive activity, not fruitfulness. Then some deep wound is sustained. A hurtful disappointment or profound sorrow become wounds of healing. Could our wounds lead us to fruitful activity?

~ISABELLE BAKER (contemporary)
Unpublished Writings

We also rejoice in our sufferings, because we know that suffering produces perseverance; perseverance, character; and character, hope.

~ROMANS 5:3

The immediate pains and sorrows do pass; but sorrow and suffering bravely borne beget a clarity of vision and a depth of understanding which are an abiding source of comfort. Mystery and grandeur lie all about us, but most of us do not discover them until trouble or suffering drives us to explore the imprisoning shell in which we have encased ourselves, and then through the crevices we glimpse the heights and depths of life, its beauties as well as its bitterness.

~RALPH W. SOCKMAN (1889-1970)
The Higher Happiness

There is nothing more painful than suffering,
and nothing more joyful than to have suffered....Suffering
makes a wise mind and an experienced man.
A man who has not suffered, what does he know?

~HENRY SUSO (1300-1365)
A Little Book of Eternal Wisdom

Though outwardly we are wasting away,
yet inwardly we are being renewed day by day.
For our light and momentary troubles are achieving for us
an eternal glory that far outweighs them all.
~II CORINTHIANS 4:16-17

God has not destined us to be rich, diseaseless, and deathless, but has given us trials, in the form of poverty, disease, the death of our friends and of ourselves—for the very purpose of teaching us to center our lives. not in wealth, health, and this temporary existence, but in serving Him.
~LEO TOLSTOY (1828-1910)
Personal Letters

If things always went wrong, no one could endure it;
if they always went well, everyone would become arrogant.
~BERNARD OF CLAIRVAUX (1090-1153)
Letters

God Is With Us Through It All

As sure as God puts his children into the
furnace of affliction, he will be with them in it.
~CHARLES H. SPURGEON (1843-1892)
Morning and Evening Devotions

Shall I tell you what supported me through all these years of exile among a people whose language I could not understand, and whose attitude toward me was always uncertain and often hostile? It was this, "Lo, I am with you always even unto the end of the world." On these words I staked everything and they never failed.
~DAVID LIVINGSTONE (1813-1873), missionary to Africa

Suffering keeps the soul humble and teaches patience.
Suffering draws and forces us to God, whether we like it or not.

~HENRY SUSO (1300-1365)
A Little Book of Eternal Wisdom

God knows best what is needful for us, and all that He does is for our good. If we knew how much He loves us, we should be always ready to receive equally, and with indifference, from His hand, the sweet and bitter; all would please that came from Him.

~BROTHER LAWRENCE (c.1605-1691)
The Practice of the Presence of God

The delight which the mariner feels, when, after having been tossed about for many a day, he steps again upon the solid shore, is the satisfaction of a Christian when, amidst the changes of this troublous life, he rests the foot of his faith upon this truth—I am the Lord, I change not" *(Malachi 3:6).*

~CHARLES H. SPURGEON (1834-1892)
Morning and Evening Devotions

Christ suffered for you, leaving you an example,
that you should follow in his steps.

~I PETER 2:21

As iron is fashioned by fire and
on an anvil, so in the fire of suffering and
under the weight of trials, our souls receive
the form which our Lord desires them to have.

~MADELEINE SOPHIE BARAT (1779-1865)

Since I know it is all for Christ's good, I am quite happy about "the thorn," and about insults and hardships, persecutions and difficulties; for when I am weak, then I am strong—the less I have, the more I depend on him.

~II CORINTHIANS 16:10 (TLB)

When the barn is full, man can live without God: when the purse is bursting with gold, we try to do without so much prayer. But once take our gourds away, and we want our God; once cleanse the idols out of the house, then we are compelled to honor Jehovah. "Out of the depths have I cried unto thee, O Lord." There is no cry so good as that which comes from the bottom of the mountains; no prayer half so hearty as that which comes up from the depths of the soul, through deep trials and afflictions. Hence they bring us to God, and we are happier; for nearness to God is happiness.

~CHARLES H. SPURGEON (1834-1892)
Morning by Morining

In the world you will have trouble.
But take heart! I have overcome the world.

~JOHN 16:33

God is the divine Artist of our lives, which will not be completed until He adds the final touch of color, the last detail. We are God's canvas, and our task is simply to receive the colors He has designed for us—the darks and the lights, the somber and the bright. Some of the details may seem meaningless until the last colors are added, but someday we will see it all—our life painting completed by the Master Artist. Only then will we see the reason for the dark background—perhaps as a contrast to the final brilliant flourish of His brush as He completes His work and our lives culminate in His glorious presence.

~AL BRYANT (contemporary)
Here's a Faith for You

Many men owe the grandeur of their lives to their tremendous difficulties. A high character might be produced, I suppose, by continued prosperity, but it has very seldom been the case. Adversity, however it may appear to be our foe, is our true friend; and, after a little acquaintance with it, we receive it as a precious thing—the prophecy of a coming joy.

~CHARLES H. SPURGEON (1843-1892)
Morning and Evening Devotions

Allen Gardiner's life as a missionary was one
of deep sufferings and privations. When he was found lying
dead, his diary was found where it had fallen from his hands,
telling of the hardships he had been through.
But the last sentence before he could write no more, was this:
"I am overwhelmed with a sense of the goodness of God."

~CLARA M. MATHESON (contemporary)
Journal

I believe the greatest blessing the Creator ever bestowed on me was when He permitted my external vision to be closed. He consecrated me for the work which He created me. I have never known what it was to see and therefore I cannot realize my personal loss. But I have had the most remarkable landscapes. The loss has been no loss to me.

~FANNY CROSBY (1820-1915), in
The Encyclopedia of 7700 Illustrations

If our world contained no difficulties to conquer, no pain to prick our ease, no suffering to call forth our compassion, no unexplained sorrows to accept in faith and love—yes, if our days were all sunshine, our lives would become a desert, our streams of sympathy would dry up, our eyes would become spiritually blind, and our natures, selfish.

~RALPH W. SOCKMAN (1889-1970)
The Higher Happiness

Trials are medicines which our gracious and
wise Physician prescribes, because we need them;
and he proportions the frequency and weight of them
to what the case requires. Let us trust his skill
and thank him for his prescription.
~JOHN NEWTON (1725-1807)
Letters

During more than forty-three years of incessant struggle, journeying to and fro throughout the world, I have never lost the assurance of Christ's living presence with me. He is not a mere vision. He is not an imaginative dream, but a living Presence, who daily inspires me and gives me grace. In him, quite consciously, I find strength in time of need.

~ROBERT E. SPEER (1867-1947), whose gifted son was cruelly murdered.

Each of us may be sure that if God sends us on
stony paths, He will provide us with strong shoes.
~MEGIDDO MESSAGE

My life is but the weaving
Between my God and me;
I only choose the colors,
He weaveth steadily
Sometimes He weaveth sorrow,
And I in foolish pride,
Forget He sees the upper,
And I the under side,
Not until each loom is silent
And the shuttles cease to fly,
Will God unroll the pattern
And explain the reason why
The dark threads are as needful
In the Weaver's skillful hand
As the threads of gold and silver
For the pattern which He planned.
And explain the reason why
~AUTHOR UNKNOWN

Sowing In Tears And Reaping With Songs Of Joy

Weeping may remain for a night, but rejoicing comes in the morning.
~PSALM 30:5

Peace is not found by escaping temptations, but by being tried by them.
~THOMAS À KEMPIS (1380-1471)
The Imitation of Christ

Why does God bring thunderclouds and disasters when we want green pastures and still waters? Bit by bit we find, behind the clouds, the Father's feet; behind the lightning, an abiding day that has no night; behind the thunder, "a still small voice" that comforts with a comfort that is unspeakable. The whole claim of the redemption of Jesus is that He can satisfy the last aching abyss of the human soul, not only hereafter, but here and now.

~OSWALD CHAMBERS (1874-1917)
In the Presence of His Majesty

We should never know the music of the harp if the strings were left untouched; nor enjoy the juice of the grape if it were not trodden in the wine-press; nor discover the sweet perfume of cinnamon if it were not pressed and beaten; nor feel the warmth of fire if the coals were not utterly consumed. The wisdom and power of the great Workman are discovered by the trials through which His vessels of mercy are permitted to pass.

~CHARLES H. SPURGEON (1834-1892)
Morning and Evening Devotions

I thank God for my handicaps, for, through them,
I have found myself, my work, and my God.

~HELEN KELLER (1880-1968)
The Story of My Life

I think that my whole life, from childhood until now, has been shaped to a purpose. The disappointments, the frustrations the wrong turnings have all shown me what is not good enough and are leading me to what is best. I had to be shown everything I thought I wanted in order to be convinced of what I truly want. I had to be humbled and straightened out by unfortunate events, by confusion and despair, by failure, before I could follow God's way.

~ANONYMOUS
Journal of an Ordinary Pilgrim

Every contradiction of our will, every little ailment, every petty disappointment, will, if we take it patiently, become a blessing....The ill-tempers of others, the slights and rudeness of the world, ill-health, the daily accidents with which God has mercifully strewed our paths, instead of ruffling or disturbing our peace, may cause His peace to be shed abroad in our hearts abundantly.

~EDWARD B. PUSEY (1800-1882)

God's most beautiful jewels are often delivered in rough packages by very difficult people, but within the package we will find the very treasures of the King's palace and the Bridegroom's love.

~ALBERT B. SIMPSON (1844-1919)
The Life of A. B. Simpson

Now for a little while you may have had to suffer grief in all kinds of trials. These have come so that your faith—of greater worth than gold, which perishes even though refined by fire—may be proved genuine and may result in praise, glory and honor when Jesus Christ is revealed.

~I PETER 1:6-7

Affliction comes to us all not to make us sad, but sober; not to make us sorry, but wise; not to make us despondent, but by its darkness to refresh us, as the night refreshes the day; not to impoverish, but to enrich us, as the plough enriches the field; to multiply our joy, as the seed, by planting, is multiplied a thousand-fold.

~HENRY WARD BEECHER (1813-1887)
Life Thoughts

Growing Deeper

Sorrow is sent by God because of his unspeakable love for us and his desire for us to draw closer to him.

~Clara M. Matheson (contemporary)
Journal

There is a divine mystery to suffering, one that has a strange and supernatural power and has never been completely understood by human reason.

~François de Fénelon (1651-1717)
Spiritual Letters

It is through the most difficult trials that God often brings the sweetest discoveries of Himself.

Author Unknown

God is ever guiding us, sometimes with the delicacy of a glance, sometimes with the firmer ministry of a grip, and He moves with us always, even through "the valley of the shadow of death." Therefore, be patient, my soul! The darkness is not your place, the tunnel is not your abiding home! He will bring you out into a large place where you will know "the liberty of the glory of the children of God."

~John Henry Jowett (1864-1928)
My Daily Meditations

The path of the Christian is not always bright with sunshine; he has his seasons of darkness and storm. There are many who have enjoyed the presence of God for a season; they have basked in the sunshine of the earliest stages of their Christian experience; they have walked among the "green pastures" by the side of the "still waters", but suddenly they find their glorious sky is clouded; in the place of sweet waters, they find troubled streams, bitter to their taste.

The best of God's children must drink from the bitter well; the dearest of His people must bear the cross. No Christian has enjoyed perpetual prosperity; no believer can always keep his harp from the willows. Perhaps the Lord allotted you at first a smooth and unclouded path because you were weak and timid. He tempered the wind for the shorn lamb, but now that you are stronger in the spiritual life, you must enter upon the riper and rougher experience of God's full-grown children. We need winds and tempests to exercise our faith, to tear off the rotten bough of self-dependence, and to root us more firmly in Christ.

~CHARLES H. SPURGEON (1834-1892)
Morning and Evening Devotions

After a time of ever-increasing joy in communion with the Lord, there often comes a time of discouragement and uneasiness when we cease to feel the presence of the Lord. Our quiet times will prove unfruitful. We will become distracted and inspirational thoughts will dry up. Our initial fervor and first joyous gifts have been taken away for a time to make room for a deeper calm and peace. The Lord our God is withdrawing from us to allow us to draw closer to Him, to seek Him with greater ardor, and having sought may find Him with greater joy.

~CATHERINE DE RAMBOUILLET (20th cent.)
Ramblings

When God hides His face from you, do not say that He has forgotten you. Waiting on Him exercises your gift of grace and tests your faith. Therefore continue to wait in hope, for although the promise may linger, it will never come too late.

~CHARLES H. SPURGEON (1834-1892)
Morning and Evening Devotions

See, I have refined you, though not as silver; I have
tested you in the furnace of affliction. For my own sake, I do this.
~ISAIAH 48:10

Lord, my God, when the storm is loud,
and the night is dark, and the soul is sad, and the
heart oppressed; then, may I look to you;
and beholding the light of your love, may it bear me on,
until I learn to sing your song in the night.
~GEORGE E. DAWSON (1861-1936)

Closing Prayer

Dear Lord, help me to see more clearly that
You love me when You allow problems to come into my life.
I am so glad You have a plan for my life. I know that You
allow difficulties to bring me to a clearer vision
and deeper understanding of Your deep purposes.
Thank you for the comforting words, "My grace is sufficient for
You: for my strength is made perfect in weakness."
Amen.

Chapter 15

Seeking A Closer Walk With God

Cultivating Gives the Soil Room to Breathe

> Prayer and faith, inseparable companions, plant a garden in the soul, and in this wondrous garden roses bloom not only in December but all the year round.
>
> ~V. L. Crawford (20th cent.)

Prayer is an expression of the inner vision, the inner music, the inner trust and commitment by which a person of faith lives. It aligns us with God's purpose. It leaves us alone with Him which brings us into a loving awareness of His Presence. It is not simply a matter of changing things externally, but one of working miracles within our inner self. It changes the way we look at things. We pray to make God's will known to us. We pray not to get more, but to be more. Prayer opens the door for self to go out and God to come in. He did not remove the "thorn" in Paul's flesh. He did something better. He gave Paul the grace to accept it and to use it to further His kingdom.

Prayer Establishes A Loving Relationship With God

Prayer is a sincere, sensible, affectionate pouring out of the soul to God, through Christ in the strength and assistance of the Spirit, for such things as God has promised.

~JOHN BUNYAN (1628-1688)
Pilgrim's Progress, in A Treasury of Sermon Illustrations

This is the high meaning of prayer—not to get things but to realize God. This is the greatest answer to prayer—not bread nor guidance, but comradeship, divine-human comradeship.

~ALBERT E. DAY (1884-1973)
An Autobiography of Prayer

Prayer is the soul's sincere desire,
Uttered or unexpressed—
The motion of a hidden fire,
that trembles in the breast.
Prayer is the burden of a sigh,
The falling of a tear,
The upward glancing of an eye,
When none but God is near.

~JAMES MONTGOMERY (1866-1674)

To pray is to desire; but it is to desire what God would have us desire.

~FRANÇOIS DE FÉNELON (1651-1717)
Advice Concerning Prayer

The spirit of prayer is a pressing forth
of the soul out of this earthly life. It is a stretching
with all its desire after the life of God.
~William Law (1686-1761)
A Serious Call to a Devout and Holy Life

Right prayer is not escape from action, it is equipment for action. It is not idle luxury, it is no luxury at all. If anyone ever really has prayed, he knows it is not! It is labor of the most demanding and disciplined variety. It is not a waste of time. The hours spent in communion with God, make better, more effective, the hours spent in action. It is not an effort to get God to do what we ought to do, but to let God equip us for the doing, and help us in the doing and finally to do all what we alone cannot do.

~Albert E. Day (1884-1973)
An Autobiography of Prayer

Prayer is a rising up and a drawing
near to God in mind, and in heart, and in spirit.
~Alexander Whyte (1836-1921)

The wish to pray is a prayer in itself.
~George Bernanos (1887-1948)
The Diary of a Country Priest

God is perfect love and perfect wisdom.
We do not pray in order to change His will,
but to bring our wills into harmony with His.
~William Temple (1821-1902)
Christian Faith and Life

Ask and it will be given to you; seek and
you will find; knock and the door will be opened to you.
For everyone who asks receives;
he who seeks finds; and to him who knocks,
the door will be opened.
~MATTHEW 7:7-8

Prayer does not consist in an effort to obtain from God the things which are necessary for this life. Prayer is an effort to lay hold of God Himself, the author of life.

~SADHU SUNDAR SINGH (1889-1929)
At the Master's Feet

Begin the day with God.
Every morning, lean thine arms awhile
Upon the window-sill of Heaven,
And gaze upon the Lord…
Then with that vision in thy heart,
Turn strong to meet the day.
~AUTHOR UNKNOWN

Prayer is not an exercise; it is the life of the saint.
~OSWALD CHAMBERS (1874-1917)
My Utmost for His Highest

The sweetest lesson I have learned
in God's school is to let the Lord choose for me.
~DWIGHT L. MOODY (1837-1899), in
A Treasury of Sermon Illustrations

"Before they call I will answer; while they are speaking I will hear" *(Isaiah 65:24).* There are no "ifs" in that verse, only certainty. Prayer to me is more than pleading. It is thanking. God has already given us everything, but we receive through prayer as we have need, according to His promise. Sometimes in those moments of quiet lifting up to God, I see the answer to something I've been trying to understand and I feel peace and renewed strength.

~CLARA M. MATHESON (contemporary)
Journal

The Lord is near to all who call on him,
to all who call on him in truth.
~PSALM 145:18

God Answers In Unexpected Ways

What discord should we bring into the universe
if our prayers were all answered. Then we should govern the world
and not God. And do you think we should govern it better?
~HENRY WADSWORTH LONGFELLOW (1807-1882), in
The Encyclopedia of Religious Quotations

Answers to prayer often come in unexpected ways. We pray, for instance, for a certain virtue; but God seldom delivers Christian virtues all wrapped in a package and ready for use. Rather he puts us in situations where by his help we can develop those virtues. The best answers to prayer may be the vision and strength to meet a circumstance or to assume a responsibility.

~C. R. FIDLEY (20th cent.)

There is no prayer so blessed
as the prayer which asks for nothing.
~OLIVER J. SIMON (1895-1956)
Faith and Experience

One obvious reason for our unanswered petitions is, of course, the ignorance of our asking. Piety is no guarantee of wisdom…Indeed, instead of calling prayers unanswered, it is far truer to recognize that "No" is as real an answer as "Yes," and often far more kind. When one considers the partialness of our knowledge, the narrowness of our outlook, our little skill in tracing the far-off consequences of our desire, he sees how often God must speak to us, as Jesus did to the ambitious woman, "Ye know not what ye ask" *(Matthew 20:22).*

~HARRY EMERSON FOSDICK (1878-1969)
The Meaning of Prayer

Prayer is a special exercise of faith. The one who prays correctly never doubts that the prayer will be answered, even if the very thing for which one prays is not given. For we are to lay our need before God in prayer but not prescribe to God a measure, manner, time, or place. He may wish to give it to us in another, perhaps better, way than we think is best.

~MARTIN LUTHER (1483-1546)
Table Talk of Martin Luther

God's way of answering the Christian's prayer
for more patience, experience, hope and love often is to
put him into the furnace of affliction.
~RICHARD CECIL (1748-1810)
Memoir, in *One Thousand New Illustrations*

He prayed for strength that he might achieve;
He was made weak that he might obey.
He prayed for riches that he might be happy;
He was given poverty that he might be wise.
He prayed for power that he might have the praise of men;
He was given infirmity that he might feel the need of God.
He prayed for all things that he might enjoy life;
He was given life that he might enjoy all things.
He had received nothing that he asked for—all that he hoped for;
His prayer was answered—he was most blessed.
~Author Unknown

Becoming Companions With God

Even as beginners we all know that the greatest thing that can happen in prayer is a sense of the presence of God. It is the possibility of this experience that makes praying such an exhilarating undertaking. The tiniest moment of feeling lifted into full harmony, of standing on the verge of grasping the meaning of life—even a fleeting experience of such wholeness is so transforming that we take up our daily tasks as if we were new persons.

~MARGUERITE HARMON BRO (1894-1977):
More Than We Are

Prayer is so necessary and the source of so
much good, that the soul which has found this treasure
cannot resist returning to it when left to itself.
~FRANÇOIS DE FÉNELON (1651-1717)
Instructions

Deep in every one of us lies the tendency to pray. If we allow it to remain merely a tendency, it becomes nothing but a selfish, unintelligent, occasional cry of need. But understood and disciplined, it reveals possibilities whose limits never have been found.

~HARRY EMERSON FOSDICK (1878-1969)
The Meaning of Prayer

Call to me and I will answer you and tell you great and unsearchable things you do not know.

~JEREMIAH 33:3

The purpose of prayer is not to change God's intention, which is already perfectly loving, but rather, by some mysterious process, which in our finiteness we cannot understand, to open channels of grace and power which otherwise are closed. If you can turn to God, at any time of day or night, as naturally and unpretentiously as a child turning to his mother, you have found the secret of the saints.

~D. ELTON TRUEBLOOD (1900-1994)

The prayer of a righteous man is powerful and effective.

~JAMES 5:16

The greatest value of prayer is not to get things or even for guidance, but for companionship with God. Prayer releases us from self-absorption to an awareness of God. Prayer allows us to be present with God, who is always present with us.

~CLARA M. MATHESON (contemporary)
Journal

Probably the greatest result of the life of prayer is an unconscious but steady growth into the knowledge of the mind of God and into conformity with His will; for after all, prayer is not the means whereby God's will is bent to man's desires, but that whereby man's will is bent to God's desires.
~CHARLES H. BRENT (1862-1929)

Watering The Garden Through Meditation

Meditation is the process of watering the garden of our soul. We feed on the Word of God and then assimilate it into our being by meditating upon it. When we need these words, we will discover that they will come up and offer themselves to us as a gift of God. We can open the secret door to our garden wherever we are—in the bustle of everyday life or the early morning quiet time. The flowers will bloom for us, the sky will be aglow with warmth.
~CATHERINE DE RAMBOUILLET (20th cent.)
Ramblings

Whatever is true, whatever is noble, whatever is right, whatever is pure, whatever is lovely, whatever is admirable—if anything is excellent or praiseworthy—think about such things.
~PHILLIPIANS 4:8

Why is it that some Christians, although they hear many sermons, make but slow advances in the divine life? Because they neglect their closets, and do not thoughtfully meditate on God's Word. They want the corn, but they will not go forth into the fields to gather it; the fruit hangs upon the tree, but they will not pluck it; the water flows at their feet, but they will not stoop to drink it.
~CHARLES H. SPURGEON (1834-1892)
Morning and Evening Devotions

Meditation is the activity of calling to mind, and thinking over, and dwelling on, and applying to oneself, the various things that one knows about the words and ways and purposes and promises of God. It is an activity of holy thought, consciously performed in the presence of God, under the eye of God, by the help of God; as a means of communion with God. Its purpose is to clear one's mental and spiritual vision of God, and to let His truth make its full and proper impact on one's mind and heart.... As we contemplate the unsearchable riches of divine mercy displayed in the Lord Jesus Christ, as we enter more and more deeply into this experience of being humbled and exalted, our knowledge of God increases, and with it our peace, our strength, and our joy.

~J. I. PACKER (contemporary)
Knowing God

So we fix our eyes not on what is seen,
but on what is unseen. For what is seen is temporary,
but what is unseen is eternal.
~II CORINTHIANS 4:18

If prayer is an asking, meditation is the listening
for an answer. And not a listening with the ears alone but
with the gathering together of one's entire being.
~MARGUERITE HARMON BRO (1894-1977)
More Than We Are

Through quiet meditation and prayer we can forget self and all
our worldly concerns and let God be present to us.
~ISABELLE BAKER (20th cent.)
Unpublished Writings

The Joy Of Walking Continually In God's Presence

I pray that out of his glorious riches he may
strengthen you with power through his Spirit in your inner being,
so that Christ may dwell in your hearts through faith.
And I pray that you, being rooted and established in love,
may have power, together with all the saints,
to grasp how wide and long and deep is the love of Christ,
and to know this love that surpasses knowledge—that you may be
filled to the measure of all the fullness of God.
~EPHESIANS 3:16-19

As soon as we are with God in faith and in
love, we are in prayer.
~FRANÇOIS DE FÉNELON (1651-1717)
Spiritual Letters

Christianity demands the absolute price. There is no finding without losing; there is no getting without giving; there is no living without dying. For a few dollars we can get a book on religion; for a few more dollars we can get some one to talk to us about the things of religion; but what we cannot get for dollars, however high we heap them, is this experience which is the heart of religion, this experience of God, this practice of the divine presence, this joy of being ourselves in the holy of holies.

~RUFUS M. JONES (1863-1948)
The World Within

Those who obey his commands live in him,
and he in them. And this is how we know that he lives in us:
We know it by the Spirit he gave us.
~I JOHN 3:24

Now that I have discovered God I find that it is a continuous discovery. Every day is rich with new aspects of him and His working. As one makes new discoveries about his friends by being with them, so one discovers the "individuality" of God if one entertains him continuously. One thing I have seen this week is that God loves beauty. Everything he makes is lovely. The clouds, the tumbling river, the waving lake, the soaring eagle, the slender blade of grass, the whispering of the wind, the fluttering butterfly, this graceful transparent nameless child of the lake which clings to my window for an hour and vanishes forever. Beautiful craft of God! And I know that He makes my thought-life beautiful when I am open all the day to Him.

~FRANK C. LAUBACH (1884-1970)
Letters by a Modern Mystic

Remain in me and I will remain in you.
No branch can bear fruit by itself: it must remain in the vine.
Neither can you bear fruit unless you remain in me.
~JOHN 15:4

Prayer satisfies our hunger for God and yet gives us greater hunger. What a divine paradox. We get what we want, but we want more. This is what calls us to "pray without ceasing," a continual hunger and being filled.

~CATHERINE DE RAMBOUILLET (20th.cent.)
Ramblings

Love God and you will always be speaking to him.
The seed of love is growth in prayer.
~JEAN-NICOLAS GROU (1731-1803)
How to Pray

I pray all the time these days. If I stopped praying, I think I'd stop living….I pray because I can't help myself. I pray because I'm helpless. I pray because the need flows out of me all the time, waking and sleeping. It doesn't change God, it changes me.

~C. S. LEWIS (1898-1963), in
Omniread Treasuries

Draw near to God and he will draw near to you.
~JAMES 4:8

As we grow in the Christian life, prayer becomes more and more real to us, and we are conscious of a progression. From prayer merely as a recourse in emergencies, and then prayer at appointed times, we move on to prayer as a state of daily living. In this last and highest development, stated times of prayer are not abandoned, but the heart does not limit itself to these in communing with God.

~JAMES R. MILLER (1840-1912)
Glimpses Through Life's Windows

It is not enough to have one contact with God. The true Christian wants to have an abiding fellowship with God. Prayer is the means of realizing this desire. Prayer, then, in its highest sense is an abiding experience of fellowship with God.

~C. E. COLTON (contemporary)
The Sermon of the Mount

Closing Prayer

Lord, I do not know what to ask of You;
only You know what I need; You love me better than
I know how to love myself. I simply open my heart to You.
I adore all Your purposes without knowing them;
I have no other desire than to accomplish
Your will. Teach me to pray.
Amen.

Chapter 16

Cherishing God's Word

The Plants Soak up Sunshine and Rain.

> One of the saddest conditions of a human creature is to read God's Word with a veil upon the heart, to pass blindfolded through all the wondrous testimonies of redeeming love and grace which the Scriptures contain. And it is sad, also, to pass blindfolded through the works of God, to live in a world of flowers, and stars and sunsets, and a thousand glorious objects of nature, and never to have a passing interest awakened by any of them.
>
> ~Edward M. Goulburn (1818-1897)
> *Thoughts on Personal Religion*

Jesus Christ is the key to understanding the whole of Scripture. From the very beginning, starting with Adam and Eve, the Bible is the story of God's redemption of mankind through Jesus Christ, the story of drawing people to experience a loving relationship with Him. The testimony of each character in Scripture clamors for us to hear and respond to the message of salvation. Jesus' voice speaks out to the deepest need of our hearts as no other voice can. He whispers our name saying, "Come unto me all of you and I will give you rest *(Matt. 11:28)*." The more we read and meditate on God's Word, the more alive it becomes. We receive exactly what we need to face the coming day.

It Is Jesus From Beginning To End

Consider the gentleness of Jesus, the purity of His morals, the persuasiveness of His teaching. How lofty His principles! What wisdom in His words! How opportune, frank and direct His answers! How can the Gospel history be an invention?

~JEAN-JACQUES ROUSSEAU (1712-1778)
Émile

The words I have spoken to you are spirit and they are life.

~JOHN 6:63

The Old Testament stopped because Jesus the Messiah had come. God didn't need to go on revealing Himself to his people as He did in the Old Testament. God's new covenant is written in people's hearts and open to all people everywhere.

~CATHERINE DE RAMBOUILLET (20th cent.)
Ramblings

The Sermon on the Mount is not a set of rules and regulations—it is a picture of the life we will live when the Holy Spirit is having His unhindered way with us.

~OSWALD CHAMBERS (1874-1917)
My Utmost for His Highest

The Bible has one theme. It is Jesus from the beginning to the end. Over 300 prophesies in the Old Testament shout out the coming of the Messiah. The more we read and understand God's Word with faith and love, the more alive it becomes. Whole passages begin to take on new meaning. The remarkable thing is that a collection of books written by forty authors over forty generations would have so much unity. The parts all fit together. Oh God, how great You are.

~ISABELLE BAKER (contemporary)
Unpublished Writings

People need more than bread for their life,
they must feed on every word of God.
~MATTHEW 4:4 (NLT)

The book of Revelation consummates the entire New Testament. It pulls away the veil and lets us look to the future. The promise of Christ's return points to the eventual conclusion of God's plan that all who trust in Him will spend eternity with Him. Thus God's plan, certain before creation began, will be perfectly complete. God will pull out all the stops and decisively defeat evil. The language is symbolic and difficult, but the message is clear. We who love Christ will be victorious. Jesus will reign forever and ever.

~CATHERINE DE RAMBOUILLET (20th cent.)
Ramblings

The Word Of The Lord Stands Forever

Scripture grows upon the student. It is full of
surprises. Under the teaching of the Holy Spirit, to the searching
eye it glows with splendor of revelation.
~CHARLES H. SPURGEON (1834-1892)
Morning and Evening Devotions

The most learned, acute, and diligent student cannot, in the longest life, obtain an entire knowledge of this one volume. The more deeply he works the mine, the richer and more abundant he finds the ore; new light continually beams from this source of heavenly knowledge, to direct the conduct, and illustrate the work of God and the ways of men; and then will at last leave the world confessing, that the more he studied the Scriptures, the fuller conviction he had of his own ignorance, and of their inestimable value.

~WALTER SCOTT (1771-1832)

God's gracious Word can make you into what he wants you to be and give you everything you could possibly need.

~ACTS 20:34 (MSG)

The Bible itself is a standing and an astonishing miracle. Written, fragment by fragment, throughout the course of fifteen centuries, under different states of society, and in different languages, by persons of the most opposite tempers, talents, and conditions, learned and unlearned, prince and peasant, bond and free; cast into every form of instructive composition and good writing, history, prophecy, poetry, allegory, emblematic representation, judicious interpretation, literal statement, precept, example, proverbs, disquisition, epistle, sermon, prayer—in short all rational shapes of human discourse; and treating, moreover, of subjects not obvious, but most difficult.

~J. M. MACLAGEN (20th cent.)

The Word of God will stand a thousand readings; and he who has gone over it most frequently is the surest of finding new wonders there.

~CLARA M. MATHESON (20th cent.)
Journal

All men are like grass,
And all their glory is like the flowers of the field;
the grass withers and the flowers fall,
but the Word of the Lord stands forever.
~I PETER 1:24-25

The Bible is a book for the mind, the heart, the conscience, the will and the life. It suits the palace and the cottage, the afflicted and the prosperous, the living and the dying. It is a comfort to "the house of mourning," and a check to "the house of fasting." It "giveth seed to the sower, and bread to the eater." It is simple, yet grand; mysterious, yet plain; and though from God, it is, nevertheless, within the comprehension of a little child.

~T. L. HAINES (20th cent.)
The Royal Path of Life

The Word of God is living and active.
Sharper than any double-edged sword, it penetrates even to dividing soul and spirit, joints and marrow;
it judges the thoughts and attitudes of the heart.
~HEBREWS 4:12

Every light that comes from Holy Scripture comes from the light of grace. This is why foolish, proud and learned people are blind even in the light, because the light is clouded by their own pride and selfish love. They read the Scripture literally, not with understanding. They have let go of the light by which the Scripture was formed and proclaimed.

~CATHERINE OF SIENA (1347-1380)
Treatise of Discretion

"For the message of the cross is foolishness to those who are perishing, but to us who are being saved, it is the power of God" *(I Cor.1:18).* The Bible becomes a new book. Whole passages begin to take on new importance. The parables come alive with new meaning. The redeeming message is clear to all who love Him.

~ISABELLE BAKER (contemporary)
Unpublished Writings

As the rain and snow come down from heaven,
and do not return to it without watering the earth and
making it bud and flourish, so that it yields seed for
the sower and bread for the eater, so is my word
that goes out from my mouth: It will not return to me empty,
but will accomplish what I desire
and achieve the purpose for which I sent it.
~ISAIAH 55:10-11

Closing Prayer

Father, let your word be
a lamp to my feet, and a light to my path.
Let me hide it in my heart that
I might not sin against you.
Amen.

Chapter 17

Understanding God's Eternal Plan

The Plant Dies, yet Its Seed Brings Forth New Life

As it is in the plant world, so it is in God's kingdom. Through death came everlasting life. Through crucifixion and the tomb came the throne of the eternal God. Through apparent defeat came victory.

~Henry Ward Beecher (1813-1887)
Life Thoughts

Although plants wither and die, the seeds they form are crammed with vitality. God created the cycle of life and set it within the heart of each tiny seed. In like manner we, too, receive the God-given promise of eternal life in Christ. Christ has conquered death through His resurrection. We know that death is only a doorway through which we, by our faith in Christ, will pass into eternal life with Him. Only God could place the reassurance of immortality within our hearts. The end of our earthly life's symphony represents a triumphant finale to what has preceded it, but, oh, the next symphony, what glory awaits us there!

God Has Set Eternity In Our Hearts

God has let us know there is life after death! He did it in the most vivid way possible: by allowing one man—Jesus Christ—to die before hundreds of witnesses, and then bringing him back to life again. Yes, there is life beyond the grave, and the proof is the resurrection of Jesus Christ. Do you want to know—really know—if there is life after death? Look at Christ, who passed through death and then came back to give us the assurance of heaven's reality.

~BILLY GRAHAM (contemporary), response to a reader's question in *The Kansas City Star*

Our Lord has written the promise of the
resurrection, not in books alone, but in every leaf in springtime.

~MARTIN LUTHER (1483-1546)
Table Talk of Martin Luther

Surely God would not have created such a being as a man, with an ability to grasp the infinite, to exist only for a day. No, no, man was made for immortality.

~ABRAHAM LINCOLN (1809-1865), in
The Encyclopedia of Religious Quotations

Now we see but a poor reflection
as in a mirror; then we shall see face to face. Now I know in part;
then I shall know fully, even as I am fully known.

I CORINTHIANS 13:12

The resurrection is the
cornerstone of the entire building of Christianity.

~CHARLES H. SPURGEON (1834-1892)
Morning and Evening Devotions

The hunger and thirst of immortality is
upon the human soul, filling it with aspirations and desires
for higher, better things than the world can give.
~TRYON EDWARDS (1809-1894), in
New Dictionary of Thoughts

*Before long, the world will not see me
anymore, but you will see me. Because I live, you also will live.*
~JOHN 14:19

Would any God who breathes in us such need
And power to learn of Him, who let us look
Upon some pages freely, bid us read
The preface only—and then shut the book?
~ADELAIDE LOVE (20th cent.)
"For a Materialist"

*Why should any of you consider it incredible that
God raises the dead?*
~ACTS 26:8

Those are dead even for this life who hope for no other.
~JOHANN WOLFGANG VON GOETHE (1749-1832)

The Bible opens with a garden. It closes with a garden. The first is the Paradise that is lost. The last is Paradise regained. And between the two there is a third garden, the garden of Gethsemane. And it is through the unspeakable bitterness and desolation of Gethsemane that we find again the glorious garden through which flows "the river of water of life." Without Gethsemane, no New Jerusalem! Without its mysterious and unfathomable night, no blessed sunrise of eternal hope! "We were reconciled to God by the death of His Son."

~John Henry Jowett (1864-1923)
My Daily Meditation

I am the resurrection and the life: he that believes in me will live, even though he dies; and whoever lives and believes in me will never die.

~John 11:25-26

The resurrection of Jesus Christ is our hope today. It is our assurance that when, in the end, we set forth on that last great journey, we shall not travel an uncharted course, but rather we shall go on a planned voyage—life to death to eternal living.

~Raymond MacKendree (20th cent.)
Queens' Gardens

I tell you the truth, whoever hears my word and believes him who sent me has eternal life and will not be condemned; he has crossed over from death to life.

~John 5:24

Death cannot kill what never dies.

~William Penn (1644-1718)
Some Fruits of Solitude

I am the Living Bread that came down from heaven.
If anyone eats of this bread, he will live forever.
~JOHN 6:51

Death is not a journeying in to an unknown
land; it is a voyage home. We are going not to a strange
country, but to our Father's house.
~JOHN RUSKIN (1819-1900)

Our bodies are like tents that we live in here
on earth, but when these tents are destroyed we know
that God will give each of us a place to live.
These homes will not be buildings that someone has made,
but they are in heaven and last forever.
~II CORINTHIANS 5:1 (CEV)

Death is not extinguishing the light; it is only putting
out the lamp because the Dawn has come.
~RABINDRANATH TAGORE (1861-1941)

God has given us eternal life, and this life is in his Son.
He who has the Son has life; he who does not have the Son of God
does not have life. I write these things to you who believe in
the name of the Son of God so that you may
know that you have eternal life.
~I JOHN 5:11-13

In the last analysis, it is our conception of death
which decides our answers to all the questions that life puts to us.
~DAG HAMMARSKJOLD (1905-1961)
Markings

Life Is But A Breath

We are like deep sea divers moving slowly and clumsily in the dim twilight of the depths, and we have our work to do. But this is not our element, and the relief of the diver in coming back to fresh air and sunlight and the sight of familiar faces is but a poor picture of the unspeakable delight with which we shall emerge from our necessary imprisonment into the loveliness and satisfaction of our true home.

~J. B. PHILLIPS (1906-1982)
Making Men Whole

All the days ordained for me were written in your book
before one of them came to be.
~PSALM 139:16

When a man surveys his past from middle age he must surely ask himself what those bygone years have taught him. If I have learned anything in the swift unrolling of the web of time, it is the virtue of tolerance, of moderation in thought and deed, of forbearance towards one's fellowmen. I have come also to acknowledge the great illusion which lies in the pursuit of a purely material goal. Above all am I convinced of the need, irrevocable and inescapable, of every human heart for God. No matter how we try to escape, to lose ourselves in restless seeking, we cannot separate ourselves from our divine source. There is no substitute for God.

~A. J. CRONIN (1896-1981)
"*Adventures in Two Worlds,*" in *Leaves from a Spiritual Notebook*

The few little years we spend on earth are only
the first scene in a Divine Drama that extends on into Eternity.
~EDWIN MARKHAM (1850-1940)

My life is ending, I know that well, but every day that is left me I feel how my earthly life is in touch with a new infinite, unknown, but approaching life, the nearness of which sets my soul quivering with rapture, my mind glowing and my heart weeping with joy.

~FEODOR DOSTOEVSKY (1821-1881)
The Diary of a Writer

We are a mist that appears for a little while and then vanishes.

~JAMES 4:14

The truest end of life is to know the life that never ends… Death is not more than a turning of us over from time to eternity.

~WILLIAM PENN (1644-1718)
Some Fruits of Solitude

If a man that is desperately sick today, did believe he should arise sound the next morning; or a man today, in despicable poverty, had assurance that he should tomorrow arise a prince; would they be afraid to go to bed?

~RICHARD BAXTER (1615-1691)
Sermons

This life is only a prelude to eternity. For that which we call death is but a pause, in truth a progress into life.

~LUCIUS ANNAEUS SENECA (c.4 B. C.-65)
Epistle XLI

My sheep listen to my voice; I know them, and they follow me. I give them eternal life; and they shall never perish; no one can snatch them out of my hand.

~JOHN 10:25

We may let go of all things which we cannot carry into eternal life. This is a deep truth, and a positive one. Surely it is not worthwhile for us to encumber our lives with the things which we can grasp at best but a little time, when we may lay hold of a thing that shall be ours for ten thousand times ten thousand years.

~ANNA R. BROWN LINDSAY (1864-1948)
What Is Worthwhile

I am a creature of a day, passing through life as an arrow through the air. I am a spirit come from God and returning to God: just hovering over the great gulf; till, a few moments hence, I am no more seen; I drop into an unchangeable eternity!

~JOHN WESLEY (1703-1791)
The Journal of John Wesley

You have made my days a mere handbreadth;
The span of my years is as nothing before you.
Each man's life is but a breath.
~PSALM 39:5

Closing Prayer

Lord, grant that I may seek rather to comfort than to be comforted, to understand than to be understood, to love than to be loved; For it is by giving that one receives, it is by self-forgetting that one finds, it is by forgiving that one is forgiven. It is by dying that one awakens to eternal life.

~FRANCIS OF ASSISI (1182-1226)

Part Six

The Giving Soul

Inviting Others to Enjoy the Garden

If all the flowers in the world were of the same color and scent, then the very face of the earth would lose its charm. The sun's rays as they pass through colored glass do not change the colors, but only bring out their varied beauty and charm. In the same way the Sun of Righteousness, both in this world and in heaven, through the God-given virtues of believers and saints continually makes manifest His unbounded glory and love.

~Sadhu Sundar Singh (1889-1929)
At the Master's Feet

Chapter 18

Loving Others

Sharing the Garden's Bounty

Love is not a plant which will flourish naturally in human soil, it must be watered from above. Love to Jesus is a flower of a delicate nature, and if it received no nourishment but that which could be grown from the rock of our hearts it would soon wither. As love comes from heaven, so it must feed on heavenly bread....Love must feed on love. The very soul and life of our love to God is His love to us.

~CHARLES H. SPURGEON (1834-1892)
Morning and Evening Devotions

Love of neighbor is the measure of love for God. It means an openness and receptivity to our fellow man, a readiness to help without reserve. The power of love was the moral of all of Jesus' parables. From genuine love spring all sympathy and help. Negativity is a cry for love. If we really understood this, how quickly we would respond with love instead of criticism. To love where one is not loved—there lies the strength that shall never fail anyone. The true test of all words and work is—are they inspired by love? This is the one thing we have to learn. "All men shall know that you are my disciples because you have love towards one another *(John 13:5)*."

It All Depends On The Heart's Love

*Love takes pleasure in the flowering of truth,
"puts up with anything, trusts God, always looks for the best, never looks back, but keeps going to the end."*
~I CORINTHIANS 13:6-7 (MSG)

Many souls get stuck among systems and particular devotions and neglect that love which is their real end.
~BROTHER LAWRENCE (c.1605-1691)
The Practice of the Presence of God

You did not choose me, but I chose you and appointed you to go and bear fruit—fruit that will last...This is my command. Love each other.
~JOHN 15:16

Love makes him hold others innocent in his heart even when he sees infirmity or fault in his neighbor; he understands that very likely all is not as it seems on the outside, but the act may have been done with a good intention.
~JOHANNES TAULER (1290-1361)
The Inner Way

It is not a question of how much we know, how clever we are, nor even how good; it all depends upon the heart's love. External actions are the results of love, the fruit it bears; but the source, the root, is deep in the heart.
~FRANÇOIS DE FÉNELON (1651-1717)
Spiritual Letters

I pray that you, being rooted in and established in love, may have power, together with all the saints, to grasp how wide and long and high and deep is the love of Christ, and to know this love that surpasses knowledge—that you may be filled to the measure of all the fullness of God.

~EPHESIANS 3:17-19

The love we give away is the only love we keep.

~ISABELLE BAKER (contemporary)

Would not the carrying out of one single commandment of Christ, 'Love one another,' change the whole aspect of the world, and sweep away prisons and workhouses, and envying and strife, and all the strongholds of the devil? Two thousand years have nearly passed, and people have not yet understood that one single command of Christ, 'Love one another'!

~MAX MUELLER (1823-1900)
Thoughts on Life and Religion

If we love each other, God lives in us and his love is made complete in us.

~I JOHN 4:12

By loving our neighbor we show our love of God. Isn't that the exact measure of our love of God? Who, then, is our neighbor? It is anyone who shows up in our life who needs our help. The good Samaritan happened to come across a man by the side of the road who had fallen among thieves and needed his help. God's love of all people is the reason for loving the one in need that He sends to us personally to minister unto. That makes it a personal act, love given person to person, not just love of people in the abstract.

~CLARA M. MATHESON (contemporary)
Journal

Jesus replied: "Love the Lord your God with all your heart and with all your soul and with all our mind. This is the first and greatest commandment. And the second is like it: 'Love your neighbor as yourself.' All the Law and the Prophets hang on these two commandments."

~MATTHEW 22:37-40

It is love that asks, that seeks, that knocks, that finds, and that is faithful to what it finds.

~ST. AUGUSTINE (354-430)

Whenever we have been blind to our neighbor's interest, we have also been blind to our own; whenever we have hurt others, we have hurt ourselves still more.

~CHARLES KINGSLEY (1819-1875)
Sermons for the Times

The surest way to determine whether one possesses love of God is to see whether he loves his neighbor. These two loves are never separated.

~TERESA OF AVILA (1515-1582)

Whoever loves his brother lives in the light, and there is nothing in him to make him stumble, but whoever hates his brother is in the darkness and walks around in the darkness; he does not know where he is going because the darkness has blinded him.

~I JOHN 2:11

Prejudices are rarely overcome by arguments;
not being found in reason they cannot be destroyed by logic.
~TRYON EDWARDS (1809-1894), in
The New Dictionary of Thoughts

We can never hate another human soul without it at the same time leaving a damaging mark on our own souls. As has been said, "Harboring anger is like taking poison and hoping the object of our anger gets sick."

~CATHERINE DE RAMBOUILLET (20th cent.)
Ramblings

We love because he first loved us. If anyone says,
"I love God," yet hates his brother, he is a liar. For anyone
who does not love his brother, whom he has seen cannot love God,
whom he has not seen. And he has given us this command:
Whoever loves God must also love his brother.
~I JOHN 4:19-21

I must love the one who hates me or I will destroy myself.
Could a man understand this paradox and still hate?
~MARGUERITE HARMON BRO (1894-1977)
More Than We Are

Whoever entertains in his heart any trace of hatred for anyone regardless of what the offense may have been, is a complete stranger to the love of God.

~MAXIMUS THE CONFESSOR (c.580-662), in
The Philokalia

I expect to pass through this world but once. Any good work, therefore, any kindness, or any service I can render to any soul, let me do it now! Let me not neglect or defer it for I shall not pass this way again.

~EDWARD, EARL OF DEVON (1497-1556)

God's Path To Tranquility

Never criticize or condemn—or it will all come back on you. Go easy on others; then they will do the same for you. For if you give, you will get! Your gift will return to you in full and overflowing measure, pressed down, shaken together to make room for more, and running over. Whatever measure you use to give—large or small—will be used to measure what is given back to you.

~LUKE 6:37-38 (TLB)

What good is it that our eyes can see and our ears can hear if our hearts are blind and deaf?

~CLARA M. MATHESON (contemporary)
Journal

Do you think you deserve credit for merely loving those who love you? Even the godless do that! And if you do good only to those who do you good—is that so wonderful? Even sinners do that much! And if you lend money only to those who can repay you, what good is that? Even the most wicked will lend to their own kind for full return!

~LUKE 6: 32-35 (TLB)

Correction does much, but encouragement does
more. Encouragement after censure is as the sun after a shower.
~JOHANN WOLFGANG VON GOETHE (1749-1832)

Do not despise others because, as it seems to you, they do not possess the virtues you thought they had: they may be pleasing to God for other reasons which you cannot discover.
~JOHN OF THE CROSS (1542-1591)
The Living Flame of Love

When the Holy Spirit controls our lives,
he will produce this kind of fruit
in us: love, joy, peace, patience, kindness, goodness,
faithfulness, gentleness, and self-control.
~GALATIANS 5:22-23 (NLT)

Search thy own heart; what
paineth thee in others in thyself may be found.
~JOHN GREENLEAF WHITTIER (1808-1891)
Complete Poetical Works of Whittier

"A cup of cold water"—a little thing! But life is made up of little things, and he who would rise to higher usefulness is wise if he cherishes the loving yet seeming trifles of daily living.
~FLOYD W. TOMKINS (20th cent.)
Allgreatquotes.com

A hurtful act toward another
represents the utter poverty we feel in ourselves.
~CLARA M. MATHESON (contemporary)
Journal

Don't get impatient with others. Remember how God dealt with you—with patience and with gentleness.
~OSWALD CHAMBERS (1874-1917)
My Utmost for His Highest

The only Christian way to respond to hate is to heap deeds of kindness upon the one who thus hates us. A love which limits itself to friends and neighbors is not love at all; it is essentially selfishness.
~C. E. COLTON (contemporary)
The Sermon on the Mount

If we had no faults, we should not take so much pleasure in noticing them in others.
~FRANÇOIS DE LA ROCHEFOUCAULD (1613-1680)

Study to be patient in bearing the defects of others, because you also have many things which others must bear. We want others strictly corrected, and are not willing to be corrected ourselves. But God has so ordered it, that we may learn to bear one another's burdens, for there is no man without defect, no man sufficient for himself.
~THOMAS À KEMPIS (1380-1471)
The Imitation of Christ

It is impossible to enter into fellowship with God when you are in a critical mood. Criticism serves to make you harsh, vindictive, and cruel, and leaves you with the soothing and flattering idea that you are somehow superior to others. Jesus says that as His disciple you should cultivate a temperament that is never critical. This will not happen quickly but must be developed over a span of time. You must constantly beware of anything that causes you to think of yourself as a superior person.
~OSWALD CHAMBERS (1874-1917)
My Utmost for His Highest

The Futility Of Judging Others

You, therefore, have no excuse, you who pass judgment on someone else, for at whatever point you judge the other, you are condemning yourself, because you who pass judgment do the same things.

~ROMANS 2:1

Our judgment of others is usually faulty and inaccurate because our own vision is marred by obstacles as great, if not greater, than those which we think we see in the lives of others. By pointing out the faults of others the critic hopes to turn the attention of others away from his own sins.

~C. E. COLTON (contemporary)
The Sermon on the Mount

Lord, help me not to despise
or oppose what I do not understand.

~WILLIAM PENN (1644-1718)
Some Fruits of Solitude

The reason we see hypocrisy, deceit, and a lack of genuineness in others is that they are all in our own hearts. The greatest characteristic of a saint is humility, as evidenced by being able to say honestly and humbly, "Yes, all those, as well as other evils, would have been exhibited in me if it were not for the grace of God. Therefore, I have no right to judge."

~OSWALD CHAMBERS (1847-1917)
My Utmost for His Highest

We try to judge people, but it cannot be done in truth because we do not know their thoughts and motives. On the outside they may appear one way, but who knows what is going on inside. We are all so different, inspired by different ideas, controlled by different circumstances and influenced by different difficulties. If we could just see the other one's point of view, we could eliminate much misery in the world. Our hearts are so delicate and yet so complex, only our Maker can know us, so let's leave all judging to Him. Let us not be so arrogant as to believe that God has given us a monopoly on the truth. If we think we are better than others, we are clinging to our love of self.

~Clara M. Matheson (contemporary)
Journal

If we would read the secret history
of our enemies, we would find in each man's
life sorrow and suffering enough to disarm all hostility.
~Henry Wadsworth Longfellow (1807-1882), in
The Encyclopedia of Religious Quotations

When the actions of a neighbor are upon the stage, we can have all our wits about us, are so quick and critical we can split a hair and find out every failure and infirmity, but are without feeling or have but very little sense of our own.

~William Penn (1644-1718)
Some Fruits of Solitude

"Let him who is without sin cast the first stone" *(John 8:7).*
These are some of the noblest and greatest
words ever uttered by human lips, or heard by human ear.
~From Countess Irma's Diary (1902-1964)

There is no true and constant gentleness without humility; while we are so fond of ourselves, we are easily offended with others. Let us often think of our own infirmities, and we shall become indulgent towards those of others.

~François de Fénelon (1651-1717)
Spiritual Letters

When I feel like finding fault I always begin with myself and then I never get any farther.

~David Grayson (1870-1946)
Adventures in Friendship

We are always wanting to change others, but the Spirit brings us back to our own inner change. Jesus had a lot to say about morality, but he was most critical, not of these who had fallen into sin through weakness, but of the self-righteous hypocrite who condemned others without seeing the "board" in his own eye. When we discover an offensive personality trait in someone else which causes us to overreact, the chances are we have become blinded to it in ourselves. We all try to hide our weaknesses because in admitting them we fear exposing ourselves to ridicule. So we point to others' mistakes, inconsistencies and wrongdoing. This, we hope, will make our own inadequacies look better. Of course, this does not work.

~Catherine de Rambouillet (20th cent.)
Ramblings

Everybody thinks of changing humanity and nobody thinks of changing himself.

~Leo Tolstoy (1828-1910)
What I Believe

First take the
plank out of your own eye, and then you
will see clearly to remove the speck from your brother's eye.
~MATTHEW 7:5

How good it would be if we could learn to be rigorous in judgment of ourselves, and gentle in our judgment of our neighbors! In remedying defects, kindness works best with others, sternness with ourselves. It is easy to make allowances for our faults, but dangerous; hard to make allowances for others' faults, but wise. "If thy hand offend thee, cut it off," are words for our sins; for the sins of others, "Father, forgive them."

~MALTBIE B. BABCOCK (1858-1901)
Thoughts for Every-Day Living

Do not judge from mere appearance; for the light laughter that bubbles on the lip often mantles over the depths of a sadness, and the serious look may be the sober veil that covers a divine peace and joy.

~EDWIN H. CHAPIN (1814-1880)

Closing Prayer

Forgive me if this day I have done or said
anything to increase others' pain. Pardon the judgmental
attitude, the unkind word, the impatient gesture, the hard and selfish
deed, the failure to show sympathy where I had the opportunity; and
enable me so to live that I may daily do something
to lessen others' burdens.
Amen.

Chapter 19

Showing Kindness To All

The Garden Fills with Fragrance from Flowers of Every Size and Color

Oh, my soul! Be as the desert flower that grows, blooms, and flourishes unseen, in obedience to God's Will, and cares not whether the passing bird perceives it, or the wind scatters the petals, scarcely formed.

~Gold Dust (19th cent.)

All the teachings of the Bible about our relationship to our fellow man can be summed up in the Golden Rule. Let us learn from the life-giving example of Jesus. His whole life was one of giving Himself to others, an unspeakable kindness of heart. Let us be kind and compassionate as Jesus was, always living for others, and not for ourselves. The kind words we speak can heal wounded hearts and lift downtrodden spirits. When we expect the best of people, they almost always live up to those expectations. If we would remember that in dealing with others we are actually dealing with the Lord Himself, how quickly we would show mercy to others.

Being Compassionate Like Christ

One of the hardest lessons to learn comes from our stubborn refusal to refrain from interfering in other people's lives. It takes a long time to realize the danger of being an amateur providence, that is, interfering with God's plan for others.

~OSWALD CHAMBERS (1874-1917)
My Utmost for His Highest

The spirit of good-will, of affection, of loving understanding, generously expressed can never fail to make a place for us in the hearts of others. Often the most austere and forbidding are most hungry for the word of friendliness or encouragement that is in our power to bestow.

~ALICE HEGAN RICE (1870-1942)
My Pillow Book

So in everything, do to others what you would have them do to you, for this sums up the Law and the Prophets.

~MATTHEW 7:12

When you defend those who are absent, you retain the trust of those present.

~STEPHEN COVEY (contemporary)
The Seven Habits of Highly Effective People

Be kind, for everyone you meet is fighting a battle.

~JOHN WATSON (1575-1645)

Sincerity includes the self-restraint which refuses to make capital of others' faults, and the charity which delights not in exposing the weakness of others.

~HENRY DRUMMOND (1851-1897)
The Greatest Thing in the World

Never listen to accounts of the frailties of others; and if anyone should complain to you of another humbly ask him not to speak about him.

~JOHN OF THE CROSS (1542-1591)
The Living Flame of Love

Love does not demand of us that we should not see the faults of others; we must in that case shut our eyes. But it commands us to avoid attending unnecessarily to them, and that we be not blind to the good, while we are so clear-sighted to the evil that exists.

~FRANÇOIS DE FÉNELON (1651-1717)
Spiritual Letters

It is not what the other person does to us that counts, it is how we allow God to see us through it.

~EUGENIA PRICE (1916-1996)
Another Day

What causes fights and quarrels among you? Don't they come from your desires that battle within you? You want something but don't get it. You kill and covet because you cannot have what you want. You quarrel and fight. You do not have, because you do not ask God. When you ask, you do not receive because you ask with wrong motives, that you may spend what you get on your pleasures.

~JAMES 4:1-3

Our characters are enriched by difficult people in our lives. Could this be one of the reasons God allows it? One thing is sure. We must not allow what others do to us alter our treatment of them.

~ISABELLE BAKER (contemporary)
Unpublished Writings

Don't criticize, and then you won't be criticized.
For others will treat you as you treat them.
~MATTHEW 7:4

Be patient with those who disagree with you. Do not condemn those who do not see things just as you do, or who think it is their duty to contradict you, whether in a great thing or a small. Beware of touchiness, of testiness, of an unwillingness to be corrected. Beware of being provoked to anger at the least criticism, and avoiding those who do not accept your word.

~JOHN WESLEY (1703-1791)
Christian Perfection

He who holds his tongue in check controls both mind and body.
~JAMES 3:2 (KJV)

It is no great matter to associate with the good and gentle: for this is naturally pleasing to all, and everyone willingly enjoys peace, and loves those best that agree with him. But to be able to live peaceably with hard and perverse persons, or with the disorderly, or with such as go contrary to us, is a grace, and a most commendable and honorable thing.

~THOMAS À KEMPIS (1380-1471)
The Imitation of Christ

If you can resist replying to an unjust criticism, and overlook it with a generous attitude, you will get a tiny glimpse of God's mercy.
~CLARA M. MATHESON (contemporary)
Journal

If someone takes unfair advantage of you, use the occasion to practice the servant life. No more tit for tat stuff. Live generously. Don't pick on people, jump on their failures, criticize their faults, unless, of course, you want the same treatment. Don't condemn those who are down: that hardness can boomerang. Be easy on people: you'll find life a lot easier.
~LUKE 6:30,37,38 (MSG)

Don't allow yourself to be upset by what people are saying about you. Let the world talk. All you need to be concerned about is doing the will of God. As for what people want, you can't please everybody, and it isn't worth the effort. One quiet moment in the presence of God will more than repay you for every bit of slander that will ever be leveled against you. Just be sure that you see only God in them. They could do nothing to you without His permission. So, in the end, it is He that tests or blesses us, using them as we have need.
~FRANÇOIS DE FÉNELON (1651-1717)
Spiritual Letters

For where you have envy and selfish ambition, there you find disorder and every evil practice. But the wisdom that comes from heaven is first of all pure; then peace loving, considerate, submissive, full of mercy and good fruit, impartial and sincere.
~JAMES 3:16-17

Look for the good in people. It heals differences, invites friendship and gives courage and confidence to the discouraged heart. This simple act of always seeing the good in everyone is so simple, so obvious, yet it escapes many of us. Even though it is, of course, good to perform kind and just acts, the best gift we can give is to be a loving and encouraging person.

~CATHERINE DE RAMBOUILLET (20th cent.)
Ramblings

He who is kind to the poor lends to the Lord.
~PROVERBS 19:17

Whoever will proudly dispute and contradict will always stand outside the door. Christ, the master of humility, manifests His truth only to the humble and hides Himself from the proud.

~VINCENT FERRER (20th cent.)
Sermons

With our neighbor there is life and death:
for if we do good to our brother, we shall do good to God;
but if we scandalize our brother, we sin against Christ.
~ANTHONY (251-356), one of the Desert Fathers

It is a very small matter to you whether the man give you your right or not; it is life or death to you whether or not you give him his. Whether he pay you what you count his debt or not, you will be compelled to pay him all you owe him. If you owe him a pound and he you a million, you must pay him the pound whether he pay you the million or not; there is no business-parallel here. If, owing you love, he gives you hate, you, owing him love, have yet to pay it.

~GEORGE MACDONALD (1824-1905), in
C. S. Lewis's *An Anthology of George MacDonald*

We Forgive Others Because God Has Forgiven The Inexcusable In Us

A forgiveness ought to be like a canceled note,
torn in two, burned up so that it can never be shown
against the man.

~DWIGHT L. MOODY (1837-1899), in
A Treasury of Sermon Illustrations

Let us look into our hearts, and see if we can forgive others.
If we can, we need not doubt but God has forgiven us.

~THOMAS WATSON (1557-1592)
The Art of Divine Contentment

*Get rid of all bitterness, rage and anger,
brawling and slander, along with every form of
malicious behavior. Instead, be kind to each other,
tender-hearted and forbearing.
Forgive one another, just as God through
Christ has forgiven you.*

~EPHESIANS 4:31-32

The best way to destroy
your enemy is to make him your friend.

~ABRAHAM LINCOLN (1809-1865), in
Encyclopedia of Religious Quotations

He who has not forgiven an enemy has not yet tasted
one of the most sublime enjoyments of life.

~JOHANN KASPER LAVATER (1741-1801)

He drew a circle that shut me out—
But love and I had the wit to win:
We drew a circle that took him in.
~EDWIN MARKHAM (1850-1940)

Settle matters quickly with your adversary.
~MATTHEW 5:25

He who cannot forgive others breaks the bridge
over which he must pass himself.
~GEORGE HERBERT (1593-1633)
Essay

My forgiveness of my brother is to be complete. No sullenness is to remain, no sulky temper which so easily gives birth to thunder and lightning. There is to be no painful aloofness, no assumption of a superiority which rains contempt upon the offender. When I forgive, I am not to carry any powder forward on the journey. I am to empty out all my explosives, all my ammunition of anger and revenge. I am not to "bear any grudge."

I cannot meet this demand. It is altogether beyond me. I might utter words of forgiveness, but I cannot reveal a clear, bright, blue sky without a touch of storm brewing anywhere. But the Lord of grace can do it for me. He can change my weather. He can create a new climate. He can "renew a right spirit within me," and in that holy atmosphere nothing shall live which seeks to poison and destroy. Grudges shall die "like cloud-spots in the dawn."

~JOHN HENRY JOWETT (1864-1923)
My Daily Meditation

And when you stand praying, if you hold anything against anyone, forgive him, so that your Father in heaven may forgive you your sins.
~MARK 11:25-26

He who wishes to revenge injuries by reciprocated hatred will live in misery.
~BARUCH SPINOZA (1632-1677)
Ethics

Closing Prayer

Dear Lord, sometimes it is difficult to love the complainer, the unforgiving one, the one who can only talk about himself, but I do the same thing. Who am I to set myself up as better than they? They all have something to teach me and ways of serving that are just as good as my own. Lord, help me to love them so they will know that You love them. You recognize my limitations. You love me in spite of my sin. Help me to do that for others. Amen.

Chapter 20

Serving Others

The Birds Find Shelter within the Garden

As the apple is not the cause of the apple tree, but a fruit of it: Even so good works are not the cause of our salvation, but a sign and a fruit of the same.

~Daniel Cawdray (fl. 1589)

Jesus calls us to be servants. As a servant, we are expected to serve all whom God sends our way in humbleness and compassion. The servant finds freedom in no longer desiring to be in charge. He who humbles himself, God exalts; he who exalts himself, God humbles; from him who searches for greatness, greatness flees; he who flees from greatness, greatness searches out! True religion is meant to be acted out. We may smugly pray and talk eloquent circles around our fellowman and not live out of love. The wise one speaks little and does much. This mysterious benefit of doing something for others brings fulfillment. It blossoms in the humble heart.

Serving As A Neighbor

One of the principal rules of religion is, to lose no occasion of serving God. And since He is invisible to our eyes, we are to serve Him in our neighbor which He receives as if done to Himself in person, standing visibly before us.

~JOHN WESLEY (1700-1791)
The Journal of John Wesley

No man has a right to lead such a life of contemplation as to forget in his own ease the service due to his neighbor; nor has any man a right to be so immersed in active life as to neglect the contemplation of God.

~ST. AUGUSTINE (354-430)
Confessions

If anyone has material possessions and sees his brother in need but has no pity on him, how can the love of God be in him?

~I JOHN 3:17

The hands that tend the sick tend Christ; the willing feet that go on errands of love, work for Christ; the words of comfort to the sorrowful and of sympathy to the mourner, are spoken in the name of Christ—Christ comforts the world through His friends.

~ARTHUR F. WINNINGTON INGRAM (1858-1946)
The Mysteries of God

Now that I, your Lord and Teacher,
have washed your feet, you also should wash
one another's feet

~JOHN 13:14

Trust God for great things; with your five loaves and two fishes,
He will show you a way to feed thousands.
~HORACE BUSHNELL (1802-1876)
The Life and Letters of Horace Bushnell

Nothing is a good work unless it is done with a good motive; and there is no motive which can be said to be good but the glory of God. He who performs good works with a view to save himself, does not do them from a good motive, because his motive is selfish. He who does them also to gain the esteem of his fellows and for the good of society, has a laudable motive, so far as man is concerned; but it is, after all, an inferior motive.

~CHARLES H. SPURGEON (1834-1892)
The New Park Street Pulpit, Vol. II

I tell you the truth, whatever you did for one of the least of these brothers of mine, you did it for me.
~MATTHEW 25:40

He who cares for neither praises nor
reproaches hath great tranquility of heart.
~THOMAS À KEMPIS (1380-1471)
The Imitation of Christ

Let us learn the lessons Christ so beautifully taught, and so faithfully exemplified. He fed all the multitude and healed all the sick that were in all their coast; and from the cross he threw out the hands of sympathy and supplication, even for the infuriated mob who were delighting in His agonies and mocking at His death….This is for our imitation for He says, if thine enemy hunger, feed him; and if he thirst, give him drink; and pray for those who despitefully use you and persecute you.

~J. B. MOODY (1838-1931)
"The Exceeding Riches of the Manifold Grace of God"

Believing in Christ as Savior is
inseparable from being a Christian to your neighbor.
~MARTIN LUTHER (1483-1546)
The Table Talk of Martin Luther

The truly devout man does not run about seeking good works, but he waits until the occasion of doing good presents itself to him. He does what in him lies to ensure success; but he leaves the care of the success to God. He prefers those good works which are obscure and done in secret to those which are brilliant and gain general admiration; but he does not shrink from these latter when they are for the glory of God and the edification of his neighbor.
~JEAN-NICOLAS GROU (1731-1803)
Manual for Interior Souls

Faith And Works Are Complimentary

Not everyone who says to me, 'Lord, Lord,"
will enter into the kingdom of heaven, but only he who
does the will of my Father who is in heaven.
~MATTHEW 7:21

Faith and works are like the
light of a candle; they cannot be separated.
~JOSEPH BEAUMONT (1616-1699)

Whatever our works are—good or evil—we are, for we are the
trees and they the fruits. They show what each of us is.
~ST. AUGUSTINE (354-430)

The hours spent in communion with God, make better,
more effective, the hours spent in action.
~ALBERT E. DAY (1884-1973)
An Autobiography of Prayer

The man who plants and the man who waters have one purpose, and each will be rewarded according to his own labor. For we are God's fellow-workers; you are God's field, God's building.
~I CORINTHIANS 3:8,9 (MSG)

A Christian should always remember that the value of his good works is not based on their number and excellence, but on the love of God which prompts him to do these things.
~JOHN OF THE CROSS (1542-1591)

God's providence is not in baskets lowered from
the sky, but through the hands and hearts of those who love him.
~GEORGE BUTTRICK (20th cent.)

By their fruit you shall recognize them.
Do people pick grapes from
the thorn bushes or figs from thistles?
A good tree cannot bear bad fruit
and a bad tree cannot bear good fruit.
~MATTHEW 7:16

The Good Samaritan did not say, "Here is the wine, and here is the oil for you"; he actually poured in the oil and the wine.
~CHARLES H. SPURGEON (1834-1892)
Morning and Evening Devotions

Suppose a brother or sister is without clothes and daily food. If one of you says to him, "Go, I wish you well; keep warm and well fed," but does nothing about his physical needs, what good is it? In the same way, faith by itself, if it is not accompanied by action, is dead.

~JAMES 2:15-17

I used to ask God to help me.
Then I asked if I might help him. I ended up by asking him to do his work through me.

~J. HUDSON TAYLOR (1832-1905), in
A Treasury of Sermon Illustrations

If you spend yourselves on behalf of the hungry and satisfy the needs of the oppressed, then your light will rise in the darkness, and your night will become like the noonday.

~ISAIAH 58:10

It Is When We Give Of Ourselves That We Truly Give

We do ourselves the most good doing something for others.

~HORACE MANN (1796-1859)

There is so much to be set right in the world, there are so many to be led and helped and comforted, that we must continually come in contact with such in our daily life. Let us only take care, that, by the glance being turned inward, or strained onward, or lost in vacant reverie, we do not miss our turn of service, and pass by those to whom we might have been sent on an errand straight from God.

~Elizabeth Rundle Charles (1828-1896), in
Daily Strength for Daily Needs

The many travelers on our way,
As we meet and touch, each day,
Let every such brief contact be
A glorious, helpful ministry;
The contact of the soil and seed,
Each giving to the other's best,
And blessing, each, as well as blest.

~Susan Coolidge (1845-1905)

Every individual will be the happier the more clearly he understands that his vocation consists, not in exacting service from others, but in ministering to others, in giving his life the ransom of many.

~Leo Tolstoy (1828-1910)
What I Believe

He who refreshes others will himself be refreshed.

~Proverbs 11:25

We send out our energies in the
service of others and there comes back to us that
which becomes the food for our souls.

~Ralph W. Sockman (1889-1970)
The Paradoxes of Jesus

You and I have an inexhaustible supply of the things people value most highly—smiles, friendliness, understanding, and appreciation. The more we give away, the more we are enriched. The greatest gifts we can give to others are not material things but gifts of ourselves. The great gifts are those of love, of inspiration, of kindness, of encouragement, of forgiveness, of ideas and ideal.

~MARGUERITE HARMON BRO (1894-1977)
More Than We Are

The most obvious lesson in Christ's teaching is that there is no happiness in having and getting anything, but only in giving. It consists in giving, and in serving others. He that would be great amongst you, said Christ, let him serve.

~HENRY DRUMMOND (1851-1897)
The Greatest Thing in the World

To give to others is but sowing seed for ourselves.

~CHARLES H. SPURGEON (1834-1892)
Morning and Evening Devotions

The service we render to others is really the rent we pay for our room on this earth. It is obvious that man is himself a traveler; that the purpose of this world is not "to have and to hold" but "to give and to serve." There can be no other meaning.

~WILFRED T. GRENFELL (1865-1940)
A Labrador Doctor

If you think you are too important to help
someone in need, you are only fooling yourself.
You are really a nobody.

~GALATIANS 6:3 (NLT)

The value of our gifts of service is diminished by our love of praise from others, desire for honor, or material profit.

~CLARA M. MATHESON (contemporary)
Journal

But when you give to the needy do not announce it with trumpets as the hypocrites do in the synagogues and on the streets, to be honored by man. I tell you the truth, they have their reward in full.

~MATTHEW 6:2-3

I gave a beggar from my little store
Of well earned gold.
He spent the shining ore, and came again and yet again
Still cold and hungry as before.
I gave the Christ, and through that Christ of mine
He found himself, a man, supreme, divine!
Fed, clothed and crowned with blessings manifold.
And now he begs no more.

~ELLA WHEELER WILCOX (1855-1919)

It is not the greatness of the help, or the intrinsic value of the gift, which gives it its worth, but the evidence it is of love and thoughtfulness.

~HUGH BLACK (1903-1942?), in
New Sermons Illustrations for All Occasions

There are different kinds of gifts, but the same Spirit. There are different kinds of service, but the same Lord. There are different kinds of working, but the same God works all of them in all men.

~I CORINTHIANS 12:4

They who have learned the way to live,
Plant wisely, though they may not reap;
And this is well, since what we give
Is all that we may hope to keep.

~MARGARET E. BRUNER (1886-1970)
"In Thoughtful Mood"

It is another's fault if he be ungrateful, but it is mine if I do not give.
~LUCIUS ANNAEUS SENECA (c.4 B.C.-65)
Epistles

We are rich only through what we give; and poor only through what we refuse and keep.
~MADAME ANNE SOPHIE SWETCHINE (1782-1859)

If you will study the history of Christ's ministry from Baptism to Ascension, you will discover that it is mostly made up of little words, little deeds, little prayers, little sympathies, adding themselves together in unwearied succession—talking with the woman at the well; going far up into the north country to talk with the Syrophenician woman; showing the young ruler the stealthy ambition laid away in his heart that kept him out of the kingdom of Heaven; shedding a tear at the grave of Lazarus; teaching a little knot of followers how to pray; preaching the Gospel one Sunday afternoon to two disciples going out to Emmaus; kindling a fire and broiling fish that His disciples might have a breakfast waiting for them when they came ashore from a night of fishing, cold, tired, and discouraged. All of these things, you see, let us in so easily into the real quality and tone of God's interest, so specific, so narrowed down, so enlisted in what is small, so engrossed with what is minute.
~CHARLES H. PARKHURST (1842-1933), in
Quotationsbook.com

The rich man is not one who is
in possession of much, but one who gives much.
~JOHN CHRYSOSTOM (347-407)
Homilies

Generosity means nothing if we give what we will never miss or what we cannot use. Jesus was moved by the sacrificial gift of the poor widow, "For they all contributed out of their abundance, but she out of her poverty has put in everything she had, her whole living" *(Mark 12:44).*
~CLARA M. MATHESON (contemporary)
Journal

Bread for myself is a material question;
bread for my neighbor is a spiritual question.
~JACQUES MARITAIN (1882-1973)
Essays

Who gives himself with his alms
feeds three—Himself, his hungering neighbor and Me.
~JAMES RUSSELL LOWELL (1819-1891), from
"The Vision of Sir Launfal" Pt. II, St. 8

Closing Prayer

Teach us, Lord,
To serve You as You deserve;
To give and not to count the cost;
To fight and not to heed the wounds;
To toil and not to seek for rest;
To labor and not to ask for any reward except
that of knowing that we do Your will.
~IGNATIUS OF LOYOLA (1491-1556)

Chapter 21

Being Thankful And Sharing The Gospel Message

The Seeds Are Scattered by the Winds

Those who have found God can only inspire
others to keep searching. They can only plant the seed and
hope the soil is right for the seeds to sprout.
~Isabelle Baker (contemporary)
Unpublished Writings

When we learn to live in a state of constant gratitude, our lives will become a continual expression of thanksgiving to the Almighty who gives us everything. Each of us for whom the world has come alive through the love of God will want others to know of our wonderful discovery. We cannot actually give God to others, but we can drop clues along the way to point them in the right direction. Every person is a unique individual, and God uses us in different ways to reveal His love to others. As we share our faith we find additional reservoirs of strength within. We must give Christ away in order to keep Him alive in our hearts. "Give and it will be given unto you" *(Matt. 7:7)."*

A Thankful Heart Blesses Others

Thanksgiving has a curative power.
The heart that is constantly overflowing with gratitude will be safe from those attacks of resentfulness and gloom that bother so many religious persons. A thankful heart cannot be cynical!

~A. W. TOZER (1897-1963)
Renewed Day by Day

We are to thank God in all things; the Lord knows what is best for us, and He is ordering the course of our life, bringing the details to pass in the time and manner of His desire. He has never made a mistake, and what He allows to come into the life of His child is for the good of that child and for our profit.

~DONALD GREY BARNHOUSE (1895-1960)
Illustrating Great Themes of Scripture

This is the day the Lord has made;
let us rejoice and be glad in it.

~PSALM 118:24

If we wish our spiritual lives to flourish we need to give a large place to gratitude. The act of thanksgiving is selfless. Thus it is related to love. "We love, because he first loved us" *(1 John 4:12).*

~CLARA M. MATHESON (contemporary)
Journal

Can I be silent?—Doth not all nature around me praise God? If I were silent, I should be an exception to the universe. Doth not the thunder praise Him as it rolls like drums in the march of the God of armies? Do not the mountains praise Him when the woods upon their summits wave in adoration? Does not the lightning write His name in letters of fires? Hath not the whole earth a voice? And shall I, can I, silent be?

~CHARLES H. SPURGEON (1834-1892)
Morning and Evening Devotions

He is a wise man who does not grieve for the things which
he has not, but rejoices for those which he has.

~EPICTETUS (1st and 2nd cent.)
Discourses

Enter his gates with thanksgiving and his
courts with praise; give thanks to him and praise his name.
For the Lord is good and his love endures forever;
his faithfulness continues through all generations.

~PSALM 100:4-5

There were ten lepers healed, and only one turned back to give thanks, but it is to be noted that our Lord did not recall His gift from the other nine because of their lack of gratitude. When we begin to lessen our acts of kindness and helpfulness because we think those who receive do not properly appreciate what is done for them, it is time to question our own motives.

~ISABELLE BAKER (contemporary)
Unpublished Writings

Thanksgiving for the past makes us trustful in
the present and hopeful for the future.
What He has done is the pledge of what He will do.

~ARTHUR C. HALL (1847-1930)

Could you work miracles, you could not do more for yourself, than by a thankful spirit, for it heals and turns all that it touches into a blessing.

~WILLIAM LAW (1686-1761)
The Works of the Rev. William Law

So then, just as you received Christ Jesus
as Lord, continue to live in him, rooted and built
up in him, strengthened in the faith as
you were taught, and overflowing with thankfulness.
~COLOSSIANS 2:6,7

Being Ready To Tell Others Of Our Hope In Christ

Always be prepared to give an answer to everyone who asks
you to give the reason for the hope that you have.
But do this with gentleness and respect.
~I PETER 3:15

The thing that amazed me was how I could have lived so long in a world that contained the Bible, and never have found all this before. Why had nobody ever told me? How could people, who had found it out, have kept such a marvelous piece of good news to themselves? Certainly I could not keep it to myself, and I determined that no one whom I could reach should be left a day longer in ignorance, as far as I could help it.

~HANNAH WHITALL SMITH (1832-1911), from her diary, in
The Unselfishness of God, Barbour Publishers

We will win the world when we realize that fellowship, not evangelism must be our primary emphasis. When we demonstrate the big Miracle of Love—they will come in. People don't go where the action is, they go where love is.

~JESS MOODY (contemporary)

This is the key. We have come into this spiritual experience. We find it in ourselves sometimes by fire or earthquake, but more often by a still small voice. It changes our way of thinking, our way of dealing with our fellow man. We then want to share it with others who are seeking something deeper and more meaningful, namely God. We see this need and having been given orders from the Lord Himself, we set out to go wherever there is a need and to share this newly found discovery.

~CLARA M. MATHESON (contemporary)
Journal

We are on the mission field every day of our lives.

~CATHERINE DE RAMBOUILLET (20th cent.)
Ramblings

The joy of finding God cannot be presented to someone else like a gift on a platter but only as a clue.

~MARGUERITE HARMON BRO (1894-1977)
More Than We Are

One who can be positively depended upon, who is faithful in the least things as well as in the greatest, whose life and character are true through and through, gives out a light in this world which honors Christ and blesses others.

~JAMES R. MILLER (1840-1912)
Glimpses through Life's Windows

Spiritual pride so often shows up in the act of trying to press our views on someone else. This sharing of the good life is treacherous business. It is a thing we cannot keep to ourselves and keep, and yet offering what we consider to be the good life to a person who does not see life with our eyes is a profitless procedure. It is like pointing out the sunrise to a man who is determined to face west; we do him no favor. In fact, he resents our retarding his westward progress. Better to wait until he wonders, in passing us, what the light can be that so glorifies our own plain countenance.

~MARGUERITE HARMON BRO (1894-1977)
More Than We Are

If Christ lives in us, controlling our personalities,
we will leave glorious marks on the lives
we touch. Not because of our lovely characters, but because of His.

~EUGENIA PRICE (1916-1996)
Make Love Your Aim

Kindness has converted more sinners than zeal, eloquence or learning. Kind words are the music of the world. They have a power which seems to be beyond natural causes, as if they were some angel's song which had lost its way and come on earth. It seems as if they could almost do what in reality God alone can do—soften the hard and angry hearts of men. No one was ever corrected by a sarcasm—crushed, perhaps, if the sarcasm was clever enough, but drawn nearer to God, never.

~FREDERICK WILLIAM FABER (1814-1863)
Life and Letter of Frederic William Faber

Looking back across the years of my life, I can see the working of a divine pattern which is the way of God with His children. When I was in "prison camp" in Holland during the war, I often prayed, "Lord, never let the enemy put me in a German concentration camp." God answered *no* to that prayer. Yet in the German camp, with all its horror, I found many prisoners who had never heard of Jesus Christ. If God had not used my sister Betsie and me to bring them to Him they would never had heard of Him. Many died, or were killed, but many died with the name of Jesus on their lips. They were well worth all our suffering. Faith is like radar which sees through the fog—the reality of things at a distance that the human eye cannot see.

~CORRIE TEN BOOM (1892-1983)
Tramp for the Lord

He who believes in Me… out of his heart will flow rivers of living water"*(John 7:38).* We are to be fountains through which Jesus can flow as "rivers of living water" in blessing to everyone. Yet some of us are like the Dead Sea, always receiving but never giving.

~OSWALD CHAMBERS (1874-1917)
My Utmost for His Highest

The most important part of our task is to tell everyone who will listen that Jesus is the only answer to the problems that are disturbing the hearts of men and nations. We shall have the right to speak because we can tell from experience that His light is more powerful than the deepest darkness.

~BETSIE TEN BOOM (1885-1944),
to her sister Corrie, both in a concentration camp

You are the light of the world. A city on a hill cannot be hidden. Neither do people light a lamp and put it under a bowl. Instead they put it on its stand, and it gives light to everyone in the house. In the same way, let your light shine before men, that they may see your good deeds and praise your Father in heaven.

~MATTHEW 5:14-16

Once the soul has set out on quest for God, its whole life becomes a petition, an asking for God Himself, and for the capacity to know God and to show Him and to interpret Him to others.

~ALBERT E. DAY (1884-1973)
An Autobiography of Prayer

Go and make disciples of all nations, baptizing them in the name of the Father and of the Son and of the Holy Spirit, and teaching them to obey everything I have commanded you.

~MATTHEW 28:19,20

Closing Prayer

Dear Lord, help me to spread your fragrance everywhere I go—let me preach you without preaching, not only by words but also by my example—by the catching force, the sympathetic influence of what I do, the evident fullness of the love my heart bears to you. Amen.

~JOHN H. NEWMAN (1801-1890)
Meditations and Devotions

Epilogue

I received the news on April 5, 2007—follicular lymphoma, a non-Hodgkin's lymphoma with fifty known kinds. It was a slow-growing cancer with no cure, but treatable. I didn't know then what was involved, but I felt a peace from God and simply prayed for His will in my life. I didn't want to miss out on His best for me, or any lessons He had prepared along the journey.

Four months after my remission in December 2007, my oncologist told me that my slow-growing lymphoma had transformed into an aggressive, fast-growing type. He stated that there was nothing else he could do and referred me to a lymphoma specialist. I was surprised. I had expected the refiner's fire to be a simpler and more comfortable process.

Was God ignoring me? Or could there be some higher, hidden purpose that I was, as yet, not aware of. I remained hopeful, knowing that God had allowed this experience in my life for a purpose. Was He, in His mercy, allowing me to go deeper into a sensitivity of His mighty ways? Perhaps He brought this struggle into my life in answer to my heartfelt prayer for a deeper, closer fellowship with Him?

> "He who has begun a good thing…In the midst of trouble, God is still busy at work in you, though he may be doing so out of your sight. God never waits too long. He is never late. Nor does He lose control. He makes no misjudgments or mistakes" (Phil. 1:6 MSG).

My transformed, fast-growing, stage 4 lymphoma had a 50% chance of being cured with a stem cell transplant. I spent weeks in the hospital after the transplant. My life seemed to be put on hold. I struggled emotionally because I could no longer fulfill my normal obligations and commitments. But in the process, I came to a greater knowledge and love of God.

What did I learn through it all? I'm gradually learning more and more about the prayer of the heart, a constant state of being before God, of realizing His Divine Presence continually, and expecting Him to speak. Prayer for me became a state of standing before God in loving conversation. I am more than ever convinced that this is the secret of the "abundant" life of which Jesus spoke.

God is speaking all the time, in many ways. Insights come whenever we are open and reflective. The problem is our eyes are closed and our ears are stopped up. "The heavens are *telling* of the glory of God; and their expanse is *declaring* the work of His hands" (Ps. 19:1 NIV).

Since the stem cell transplant, my cancer has relapsed twice and I have spent several more weeks in the hospital. My greatest lesson during the last stay was: "Wait patiently on the Lord." I always thought that meant wait and delay until the Holy Spirit gives you the final word. It doesn't. It means depend upon the Lord now, trust Him, don't delay.

This sensitivity to God's presence is instrumental in developing the art of "noticing," of observing. It becomes a state of actively looking for God's presence and grace. As I work at "noticing," I begin to "see" more, to enjoy more of the simple things, and to celebrate life more. This has been one of the greatest outcomes of my "spiritual retreats." At the beginning of each "spiritual retreat" at the hospital, I was already anticipating something greater to come.

> "You know everything I want to say before I start the first sentence. I look behind me and you're there, then up ahead and you're there, too—your reassuring peace coming and going. This is too much, too wonderful. I can't take it all in!" Ps. 139:4-6 (MSG).

I can't explain His mysterious ways, but I know that His way is always right. "My grace is sufficient for you for my power is made perfect in weakness" (II Cor. 12:9 NIV). Think of that: strength in weakness, power in pain. What a beautiful paradox. It's all part of the abundant life of which Jesus speaks. It completely defies human reasoning.

> "Oh, the depth of the riches both of the wisdom and knowledge of God! How unsearchable are His judgments and unfathomable His ways" (Rom. 11:33 NAS).

I was an independent person. I had what I needed. I prided myself on having everything under control. God, in His mercy, had to remove this self-reliance for me to find a real understanding of the abundant life. God cannot pour His riches into hands already full.

When everything is going smoothly, when the pantries are full, when the sun is shining, we learn little. It is difficult to stop and listen carefully to what God is saying.

This whole experience has been challenging, with more complications still on the horizon, but it has allowed me to discover the unshakable truth that God is my strength and power. "I will sing to the Lord for He has been good to me" (Ps. 13:6 NIV).

Compiling this collection has given me great joy. It has clarified my own spiritual journey. My prayer is that the reader will gain insights from my journey that will be useful for his own journey, as we share the flowers from our spiritual gardens.

Index

D

E

F

G

H

I

J

K

S

T

U

V

W

Y

Credits And Acknowledgements

AuthorHouse Inc. expresses its appreciation to all those who generously gave permission to reprint and/or adapt copyrighted material. Diligent effort has been made to identify, locate, and contact copyright holders, and to secure permission to use copyrighted material. If any permission or acknowledgments have been inadvertently omitted the author would sincerely appreciate receiving complete information so that correct credit can be given in future editions.

1. Albright, Catherine M., comp. *Inner Light, First Series, A Devotional Anthology.* London: George Allen and Unwin, 1931.
2. Amiel, Henri-Frederic. *Private Journal*, trans. into English by Mary A. Ward.
3. *Anonymous, Journal of an Ordinary Pilgrim*. Philadelphia: Westminster, 1954.
4. Applegarth, Margaret T., comp. *Heirlooms*. New York: Harper, 1967.
5. Augustine, St. *Confessions of St. Augustine*. New York: Penguin Books.
6. Barbour, R. W., *Thoughts*, New York: Blackwood, n.d.
7. Barrett, Eric C. and David Fisher, eds. *Scientists Who Believe: 21 Tell Their Own Stories.* Chicago: Moody, 1984.
8. Barton, F. M., comp. *One thousand Thoughts for Funeral Occasions, Illustrations, Poetical Selections, Texts, with Outlines and Suggestions*. Cleveland, Ohio: F. M. Barton, 1912.
9. Beecher, Henry Ward. *A Treasury of Illustration by Henry Ward Beecher, edited from his published works and unpublished reports of his spoken words* by John R. Howard and Truman J. Ellinwood, Westwood, NJ: Fleming H. Revell Company, 1904. Reprint in *A Treasury of Illustration by Henry Ward Beecher*. London: J. B. Ford & Co., 1875.
10. Beecher, Henry Ward. *Life Thoughts, Gathered from the Extemporaneous Discourses of Henry Ward Beecher*. Boston: Phillips, Sampson, 1858.
11. Beyer, Douglas. *Parables for Christian Living*, used with permission from Judson Press. Copyright © 1985 by Judson Press.

12. Bettenson, Oxford University Press; 1970, in *A Treasury of Sermon Illustrations*, ed. Charles Wallis. Nashville: Abingdon. 1952.
13. Black, Hugh in *New Sermon Illustrations for All Occasions*, G. B. F. Hallock. Westwood, NJ: Fleming H. Revell Co., 1957.
14. Blackaby, Henry T. and Claude V. King. *Experiencing God: How to Live the Full Adventure of Knowing and Doing the Will of God.* Nashville: Broadman, 1994, used with permission.
15. Blackburn, E. A., comp. *A Treasury of the Kingdom.* NY: Oxford University Press, 1954.
16. Bonaventure. *Intinerarium Mentis in Deum. The Journey of the Mind to God.* Indianapolis: Hackett, 1993.
17. Bonhoeffer, Dietrich. *The Cost of Discipleship. New York:* Macmillan 1966, used with permission.
18. Boom, Corrie ten. *Tramp for the Lord*, used with permission from Baker Books. Copyright © 1974 by Grand Rapids: Baker Books.
19. Bro, Marguerite Harmon. *More Than We Are*, used with permission from Harper. Copyright © 1948 by New York: Harper.
20. Brother Lawrence. *The Practice of the Presence of God*, based on the conversations, letters, ways, and spiritual principles of Brother Lawrence, as well as on the writings of Joseph De Beaufort, trans. by E. M. Blaiklock. Nashville: Thomas Nelson, 1981.
21. Brooks, Phillips, in *The New Encyclopedia of Christian Quotations*, comp., Mark Waters. Grand Rapids: Baker, 1973.
22. Brown, Joan Winmill, ed. *Joy in His Presence*. Minneapolis, Minn.: World Wide Publications, 1982.
23. Bunyan, John. *Pilgrim's Progress*, in *A Treasury of Sermon Illustrations*, comp. Charles L. Wallis. ed. Charles Wallis. Nashville: Abingdon. 1952.
24. Caussade, Jean-Pierre de. *Self Abandonment to the Divine Providence*, trans. by James Beevers, used with permission from Image Books. Copyright ©1975 by Image Books.
25. Cecil, Richard, *Memoir*, in *One Thousand New Illustrations*, ed. Aquilla Webb. NY: Harper & Row, 1921.
26. Chambers, Oswald. *My Utmost for His Highest* Dodd, Mead, 1935, used with permission from Discovery House, edited by James Reimann Copyright © 1992 by Grand Rapids: Oswald Publications Association.
27. Charles, Elizabeth Rundle, in *Daily Strength for Daily Needs*, comp., Mary W. Tileston. Old Tappan, New Jersey: Revell, 1966.
28. Chervin, Ronda De Sola. *Quotable Saints*. Ann Arbor, Mich.: Servant Publications, 1992.
29. Clark, Thomas Curtis, and Hazel Davis Clark, comps. and eds. *The Golden Book of Immortality*. New York: Association Press, 1954.
30. *Cloud of Unknowing, The*. Author unknown. Translated by Ira Progoff, New York: Julian, 1957.
31. Coleridge, Samuel Taylor, in *I Quote: A Collection of Ancient and Modern Wisdom and Inspiration*, comp. Virginia Ely. New York: George W. Stewart, 1947.

32. Colson, Charles W. *Life Sentence.* Old Tappan, NJ: Fleming H. Revell © 1979. Originally published by Chosen Books: Lincoln, VA 22078
33. Colton, C. E. *The Sermon on the Mount,* Grand Rapids: Zondervan, used with permission from the author. Copyright © 1960 by C.E. Colton.
34. Covey, Stephen. *The Seven Habits of Highly Effective People,* used with permission from Simon & Schuster, Inc. Copyright © 1989 by Stephen R. Covey.
35. Cowman, L. B. *Streams in the Desert,* 1925. New edition, ed. by Jim Reimann, Grand Rapids: Zondervan, 1997.
36. Compton, Arthur H., in *Knight's Illustrations for Today,* ed. by Walter B. Knight, Chicago: The Moody Bible Institute of Chicago, 1970.
37. Cronin, A J., "Adventures in Two Worlds," in *Leaves from a Spiritual Notebook,* ed. Thomas Kepler. Nashville: Abingdon. 1960.
38. Paul Lee Tan, Dallas, Texas: Bible Communications, 1979.
39. Cushman, Ralph S. *Hilltop Verses or Spiritual Hilltops: A Book of Devotions.* Nashville: Abingdon, 1932.
40. Detherage, May. *Sunrise to Sunset: An Anthology of Man's Day in Prose and Poetry.* Nashville: Abingdon, 1966.
41. Day, Albert. *An Autobiography of Prayer,* used with permission from the Disciplined Order of Christ. Copyright © 1952 by Disciplined Order of Christ.
42. Day, Albert E. *Discipline and Discovery,* used with permission from the Disciplined Order of Christ. Copyright © 1962, 1968 by Disciplined Order of Christ.
43. Doren, Carl van. *The Oxford Dictionary of Quotations,* intro. by Carl van Doren. London: Oxford University Press, 1941
44. Dostoevsky, Feodor. *The Diary of a Writer,* trans. by Dnevnik Pisatelia. London: Cassell, 1949.
45. Dresner, Samuel. *Three Paths of God and Man,* used with permission from Harper. Copyright ©1960 by Harper, New York: Harper, 1060.
46. Drummond, Henry. *The Greatest Thing in the World,* in *Encyclopedia of Religious Quotations,* comp. Frank S. Mead: Westwood, N. J. Revell, 1967.
47. Eckhart, Meister. *Meister Eckhart Speaks: A Collection of the Teachings of the Famous German Mystic,* trans. by Elizabeth Strakosh. Copyright © 1957. Used with permission from Blackfriars: London, 1957.
48. Edwards, Tryon, comp. *New Dictionary of Thoughts: Cyclopedia of Quotations.* Revised and enlarged by C. N. Catrevas, Jonathan Edwards, and Ralph Emerson Browns. USA: Standard, 1960.
49. Ely, Virginia, comp. *I Quote: A Collection of Ancient & Modern Wisdom & Inspiration.* New York: George W. Stewart, 1947.
50. Emerson, Ralph Waldo, *Journal,* in *The Christian Reader,* ed, Stanley I. Stuber. New York: Association, 1952.
51. Epictetus, *Discourses,* trans. by P. E. Matheson. Oxford: Clarendon, 1916..
52. Fénelon, François. *Instructions in the Divine Life of the Soul.* Philadelphia: E. Jones, c1860.

53. Fénelon, François de. *Selections from the Writings of Fénelon, by a Lady*, 2nd ed. Boston: 1829.
54. Fénelon, François de. *Spiritual Letters of Archbishop Fénelon,* trans. by H. L. Lear. London: Longmans, 1909.
55. Finney, Charles G. *Memoirs of Rev. Charles G. Finney*. New York: Revell, 1908, © 1903.
56. Finley, James. *The Awakening Call: Fostering Intimacy with God.* Notre Dame, Ind.: Ave Maria, 1984. Used with permission of author.
57. Fisk, Randall, "*Beyond Einstein,*" in *Scientists Who Believe, 21 Tell Their Own Stories*, ed. Eric C. Barrett and David Fisher, *Chicago*: Moody, 1984.
58. Fosdick, Harry Emerson. *On Being a Real Person, Treasury of the Christian Faith*, comp., Stanley L. Stuber. New York: Association Press, 1949.
59. Foster, Elon, ed. *6000 Sermon Illustrations.* Grand Rapids: Baker, 1952.
60. Francis, St., de Sales. *Introduction to the Devout Life*. London: Burns, Oates, & Washbourne, 1943.
61. Geiger, Eric, *Identity: Who You Are in Christ*. Broadman & Holman: Nashville, TN, 2008, used with permission of author.
62. Gilbert, Josiah H. ed. *Three Thousand Selected Quotations from Brilliant Works.* Hartford: S. S. Scranton, 1918.
63. Gillespie, V. Barclay. *The Dynamics of Religious Conversion* by V. Bailey Gillespie. Birmingham, Al.: Religious Educational Press, 1991.
64. Gottschall, A. H., comp. *Selections from Latter Testimonies and Dying Words of Saints and Sinners: Being the Closing Expressions of Nearly Seventeen Hundred Persons, Believers and Unbelievers*. Harrisburg, Penn: "The Old Path", 1900.
65. Grayson, David. *Adventures in Friendship*. Garden City, N Y: Doubleday, 1910.
66. Grenfell, William of Labrador. *A Labrador Doctor* (his autobiography), in *A Treasury of Sermon Illustrations*, ed. by Charles L. Wallis. Nashville: Abingdon, 1950.
67. Grou, Jean-Nicolas. *Spiritual Maxims*, Springfield, Ill.: Templegate, 1961.
68. Grou, Nean-Nicolas. *Manual for Interior Souls*. Westminster: Newman, 1955.
69. Grou, Jean-Nicolas. *How to Pray: The chapters on prayer taken from the School of Jesus Christ.* New York: Harper and Brothers, 1933.
70. Happold, F. C. *Journey Inwards.* Copyright © by the estate of F. C. Happold
71. Havergal, Francis Ridley, in *The Doubleday Christian Quotation Collection*, comp. Hannah Ward. New York: Doubleday, 1997.
72. Haydn, Joseph, in the *Spiritual Lives of Great Composers*, and in *Knight's Treasury of Inspiration*, ed. Walter B. Knight. Chicago: Moody 1970.
73. Hembree, Ron. *Fruits of the Spirit*, used with permission from Baker House. Copyright © 1969 by Baker Book House.
74. Herman, Emily. *Creative Prayer*. Cincinnati: Forward Movement Miniature, n. d. (c1934).
75. Herman, Emily. *The Secret Garden of the Soul.* New York: Harper, 1924, in *Leaves from a Spiritual Notebook.* Thomas Kepler, comp. Nashville: Abingdon, 1960.

76. Hewitt, James S., ed. *Illustrations Unlimited: A Topical Collection of Hundreds of Stories, Quotations, and Humor for Speakers, Writers, Pastors and Teachers.* Wheaton, Ill.: Tyndale, 1988.
77. Holdcraft, Paul E. comp. *Cyclopedia of Bible Illustrations*. New York: Abingdon, 1947.
78. Holland, John. *John Holland's Scrapbook.* Chicago: Prairie Press, 1944.
79. Hugo, Victor, in *Treasury of Courage and Confidence,* ed. Norman Vincent Peale. Pawling, New York: Foundation for Christian Living, in association with Doubleday, 1970.
80. John, St., of the Cross. *The Ascent of Mount Carmel.* New York: Triumph Books, 1991.
81. John, St., of the Cross. *The Living Flame*. In *The Complete Works Saint John of the Order of Our Lady of Mount Carmel.* London: Longman, Green, Longman, 1864.
82. Johnson, Joseph S., comp. *A Field of Diamonds*. Nashville: Broadman, 1974.
83. Johnson, Raynor C. *The Imprisoned Splendor*, used with permission from Hodder & Stoughton Ltd. Copyright ©1953.
84. Jones, Rufus M. *The Inner Life* by Rufus M. Jones used with permission from Mary Hoxie Jones. Copyright ©1916 by Mary Hoxie Jones.
85. Jones, Rufus M. *The Eternal Goodness: A Symposium of Faith by Joseph Fort Newton;* NY: Little, Brown, and Company, 1926.
86. Jones, Rufus M. *The Eternal Gospel.* New York: Macmillan, 1938.
87. Jones, Rufus M. *The Testimony of the Soul.* New York: Macmillan, 1936.
88. Jones, Rufus M. *The World Within*. New York: Macmilllan, 1918.
89. Jowett, John Henry, in *Knight's Illustrations for Today*, ed. Walter B. Knight. Chicago: Moody, 1970.
90. Keller, Helen. *The Story of My Life. "In the Garden of the Lord":* New York: Doubleday, 1903.
91. Kepler, Thomas S. *Leaves from a Spiritual Notebook.* Thomas Kepler, comp. Nashville: Abingdon, 1960.
92. Kempis, Thomas à. *The Imitation of Christ.* Garden City, N Y: Doubleday, 1955.
93. Kennedy, Gerald, comp. *A Second Reader's Notebook.* New York: Harper, 1959.
94. Kerr, Hugh T. and John Mulder. *Famous Conversions*, used with permission from William B. Eerdmans Publishing Company.
95. Knight, Walter B., ed. *Knight's Illustrations for Today*. Chicago: Moody, 1970.
96. Knight, Walter B., ed. *Knight's Master Book of NEW Illustrations*. Grand Rapids: Eerdmans, 1956.
97. Laubach, Frank, *Letters form a Modern Mystic*, used with permission from Laubach Literacy International.
98. Law, William. *A Serious Call to a Devout and Holy Life: Adapted to the State and Conditions of All Orders of Christians*. Grand Rapids: Eerdmans, 1966.
99. Law, William. *An Appeal to All that Doubt, or Disbelieve the Truths of the Gospel*, in *The Works of the Reverend William Law*. Brockenhurst, Hampshire: Privately rep. for G. Moreton, 1892.

100. Law, William. *The Spirit of Prayer*, trans. by Stephen Hobhouse. New York: Harper, 1948.
101. Lawson, J. Gilchrist, ed. *Greatest Thoughts about Jesus Christ*. New York: Richard Smith, 1930.
102. Lewis, C. S., *Mere Christianity*. Copyright © C. S, Lewis, 1942, 1943, 1944, 1952, The Macmillan Company, used with permission.
103. Lincoln, Abraham, in *Encyclopedia of Religious Quotations*, comp. Frank S. Mead. Westwood, NJ: Revell, 1965.
104. Lindsay, Anna R. Brown. *What Is Worth While*. New York: Crowell, 1893. In *The Compact Treasury of Inspiration*, New & revised edition, ed. Kenneth Seeman Giniger. Nashville: Abingdon, 1964.
105. Livingstone, David, in *Encyclopedia of Religious Quotations*, comp. Frank S. Mead. Westwood, N. J.: Revell, 1965.
106. Longfellow, Henry Wadsworth, in *The Encyclopedia of Religious Quotations*, ed. and comp. Frank S. Mead. Westwood, N.J.: Revell, 1965.
107. Lousman, Jack in *Scientists Who Believe: 21 Tell Their Own Stories*. Chicago: Moody, 1984.
108. Luther, Martin. *Table Talk of Martin Luther,* trans. by Thomas S. Kepler. Grand Rapids: Baker, 1952.
109. Luther, Martin, in *Joy in His Presence*, ed. Joan Winmill Brown. Minneapolis, MN: World Wide Publications, 1982, used with permission of compiler.
110. Macartney, Clarence E. *Macartney's Illustrations: Illustrations from the Sermons of Clarence E. Macartney*. New York: Abingdon, 1945.
111. MacDonald, George. *Annals of a Quiet Neighborhood*. New York: G. Routeledge, 1873.
112. MacDonald, George. *Unspoken Sermons*, Third Series, Eureka, Ca.: J. Joseph Flynn Rare Books in association with Sunrise Books, 1889.
113. MacDonald, George. *Within and Without*. New York: Scribner's, 1872, in *Encyclopedia of Religious Quotations*, ed. Frank S. Mead. Westwood, N.J.: Revell, 1965.
114. Marshall, Peter. *Mr. Jones, Meet the Master*, used with permission from Baker Book House. Copyright © 1950 by Fleming H. Revell Publishers.
115. McClure, J. B., comp. *Pearls from Many Seas: A Galaxy of Thought from 400 Writers of Wide Repute*. Rhodes & McClure, 1940.
116. Frank S. Mead, ed, and comp. *Encyclopedia of Religious Quotations*. Westwood, N. J.: Revell, 1965.
117. Merton, Thomas, *New Seeds of Contemplation*. Copyright © 1961 by the Abbey of Gethsemani, Inc., used with permission of New Directions Publications, Corp.
118. Merton, Thomas, *Seeds of Contemplation*. Copyright © 1949 Our Lady of Gethsemene Monastery, used with permission of New Directions Publishing Corp.
119. Meyer, Frederick B. in "*The Illustrator,*" in *The Call and Challenge of the Unseen*. New York: Revell, 1926.

120. Miller, Ernest R., illus. by Dorothy Peebles. *Harvest of Gold*. Norwalk, Conn.: C. R. Gibson, 1973.
121. Miller, James R. *Glimpses Through Life's Windows: Selections from the Writings of J. R. Miller*. New York: Crowell, c1893.
122. Moody, Dwight, in *A Treasury of Sermon Illustrations*. Nashville: Abingdon, 1950. ", ed. Charles Wallis," after A Treasury of Sermon Illustrations, Nashville: Abingdon, 1950.
123. Morris, Thomas V., ed. *God and the Philosophers: The Reconciliation of Faith and Reason*. New York: Oxford University Press, 1994.
124. Mueller, Friedrich Max. *Thoughts on Life and Religion*. New York: Doubleday & Page, 1905.
125. Murray, Andrew, in *The Life of Andrew Murray of South Africa*, ed. J. DuPlessis, in *The Lunn Family*.
126. Nasby, A. Gordon, comp. and ed. *Treasury of the Christian World*. New York: Harper, 1953.
127. Newman, John Henry. *Meditations and Devotions*. London: Longmans, 1908.
128. Newman, John Henry. *Parochial and Plain Sermons*. London: Longmans, 1900-02.
129. Newton, John. "*Amazing Grace*" first printed in Newton's Olney Hymns in Three Parts.
130. Osborn, George, in *Knight's Treasury of Illustrations*, ed. Walter B. Knight. Grand Rapids: Eerdmans, 1947.
131. Parker, Joseph. *The Inner Life of Christ as Revealed in the Gospel of Matthew*, Vol. II. London: Richard Clark, 1881-2.
132. Packer, J. I. *Knowing God*. Downer's Grove, IL: InterVarsity Press, 1993.
133. Pascal, Blaise. *Thoughts: Selections from the Thoughts*, ed. and trans. by Arthur H. Beattie. New York: Appleton-Century-Crofts, 1965.
134. Peale, Norman Vincent, comp. *Treasury of Joy & Enthusiasm*. Pawling, New York: Foundation for Christian Living, 1981.
135. Penn, William. *The Peace of Europe: The Fruits of Solitude and the Writings by William Penn*. London: J. M. Dent, n.d.
136. Pepper, Margaret, comp. *The Harper Religious and Inspirational Quotation Companion*. New York: Harper, 1989.
137. Price, Eugenia. *Another Day*. Garden City, N. J.: Doubleday, 1984.
138. Reinhold, H. A., ed. *The Soul Afire: Revelations of the Mystics*. New York: Pantheon, 1944.
139. Rice, Alice Hegan. *My Pillow Book*. New York: Appleton-Century, 1937, used with permission from Ameron Ltd. of Mattituck, NY.
140. Richards, Edith, R., comp. *Inner Light, Second Series: A Devotional Anthology*. London: George Allen & Unwin, 1936.
141. Russell, A. J. *God at Eventide* ed. by A. J. Russell, used with permission by Arthur Jones Ltd. Copyright © 1950 by Arthur Jones Ltd.
142. Seneca, Lucius Annaeus. *"Epistle XLI"*, trans. by R. M. Gummere. Philadelphia: J. B. Lippincott, 1887.
143. Simpson, A. B., in *The Life of A. B. Simpson*, written by A. E. Thompson.

144. Singh, Sadhu Sundar. *At the Master's Feet: Meditations on Various Aspects of the Spiritual Life*. London: Macmillan, 1926.
145. Singh, Sadhu Sundar. *With and Without Christ: Being Incidents Taken from the Lives of Christians*. New York: Harper, 1929.
146. Smith, Hannah Whitall. *The Christian's Secret of a Happy Life*. New York: Revell, 1877.
147. Smith, Hannah Whitall. *The Unselfishness of God*. Uhrichsville, Ohio: Barbour, 1993. Used by permission of Barbour.
148. Sockman, Ralph W. *The Higher Happiness*. Nashville: Abingdon, 1950.
149. Sockman, Ralph W. *The Paradoxes of Jesus*, Abingdon-Cokesbury Press, 1936.
150. Soper, David Wesley, ed. *These Found the Way: Thirteen Converts to Protestant Christianity*. Philadelphia: Westminster, 1951.
151. Speer, Robert E. *"What Jesus Does for Me,"* in *"Remember Jesus Christ" and Other Talks about Church and the Christian Life."* New York: Revell, 1899.
152. Spurgeon, Charles H. *Morning and Evening Devotions: Daily Readings*. Lynchburg, VA: The Old Time Gospel Hour.
153. Stevenson, Robert Louis in *Knight's Illustrations for Today*. Chicago: Moody, 1970.
154. Stuber, Stanley I., and Thomas Curtis Clark, eds. *Treasury of the Christian Faith*. New York: Association, 1949.
155. *Sunshine for Shut-Ins*, comp. by a "shut-in". New York: Crowell, 1895.
156. Taylor, J. Hudson, in *A Treasury of Sermon Illustrations*, ed. Charles Wallis. Nashville: Abingdon. 1950.
157. Tan, Paul Lee Tan, ed. *Encyclopedia of 7700 Illustrations*. Dallas, Texas: Bible Communications, 1979.
158. Tauler, Johannes. *The Inner Way: Sermons*. New York: Paulist Press, 1985.
159. Taylor, Jeremy. *Holy Living and Dying*. rev. and ed. by the Rev. Thomas Smith. London: Henry G. Bohn, 1852.
160. Tennyson, Alfred Lord, in *One Thousand New Illustrations,* ed. Aquilla Webb.
161. Teresa, Ste., of Avila. *Interior Castle*. London: Sands, 1946.
162. Teresa, Ste., of Avila. *The Way of Perfection*. London: Thomas Baber, 1919.
163. Teresa, Ste., of Avila, in *OmniRead Treasuries*, comp. Peter Sumner. All *OmniRead Treasuries* used by permission.
164. Thurman, Howard. *Disciplines of the Spirit*. New York: Harper, 1963, used with permission of Friends United Press.
165. Tileston, Mary Wilder, comp. *Joy and Strength*. Minneapolis: World Wide Publications, 1901.
166. Tolstoy, Leo. *The Collected Works of Leo Tolstoy*. New York: Crowell, 1899.
167. Tolstoy, Leo. *What I Believe*, in *Lift Up Your Eyes*, New York: The Julian Press, Inc. 1960.
168. Tournier, Paul. *The Adventure of Living*. New York: Harper & Row.
169. Tozer, A. W. *The Pursuit of God: The Human Thirst for the Divine*, used with the permission of Christian Publications, Inc. Copyright © 1982, 1993 by Christian Publications, Inc, Camp Hill, PA 17011.

170. Tozer, A. W. *Renewed Day by Day*. Camp Hill, Pa.: Christian Publishers, 1948, used by permission.
171. Trueblood, D. Elton. *The Essence of Spiritual Religion*. New York: Harper, 1936.
172. Trueblood, D. Elton. *The New Man for Our Time*. New York: Harper, 1970.
173. Underhill, Evelyn. *Practical Mysticism: An Aspiring Introduction to the World of the Mystic*. New York: E. P. Dutton., 1915.
174. Underhill, Evelyn. *The Spiritual Life*. London: Hodder & Stoughton, 1937.
175. Underhill, Evelyn. *Fruits of the Spirit*, London: Cassell-Mowbray Ltd.
176. Wallis, Charles L., ed. *The Treasure Chest; A Heritage Album Containing 1064 Familiar and Inspirational Quotations, Poems, Sentiments, and Prayers from Great Minds of 2500 Years*. New York: Harper, 1965.
177. Wallis, Charles L., ed. *Words of Life: A Religious and Inspirational Album Containing 1100 Quotations from the Minds and Hearts of Writers of Twenty Centuries and Illustrated by Scenes of the Holy Land*, New York: Harper, 1966.
178. Wallis, Charles L., ed. *A Treasury of Sermon Illustrations*. Nashville: Abingdon, 1950.
179. Ward, Hannah, and Jennifer Ward, comps. *The Doubleday Christian Quotation Collection*. New York Doubleday, 1997.
180. Water, Mark, comp. *The New Encyclopedia of Christian Quotations*. Grand Rapids: Baker, 1973.
181. Watson, Lillian Eichler, ed. *Light from Many Lamps*. New York: Simon & Schuster, 1951.
182. Watson, Thomas. *The Art of Divine Contentment*, Glasgow, United Kingdom: Free Presbyterian Publications, n.d.
183. Webb, Acquilla, ed. *One Thousand New Illustrations* , New York: Harper and Bros., 1921.
184. Wesley, John. *The Letters of the Rev. John Wesley*. London: Epworth Press, 1931.
185. Whittier John Greenleaf. *Complete Poetical Works of Whittier*, comp. by Horace D. Scudder. Cambridge edition. Boston: Houghton Mifflin, 1894.
186. Wilson, Thomas. *Maxims of Piety and Christianity*, ed. Frederic Relton, A.K.C., Vicar of St. Andrews, Stoke Newington: London, 1898.
187. Woolman, John. *Journal and Essays of John Woolman*. New York: Macmillan, 1922.
188. Yelchaninov, Alexander. *Fragments of a Diary*, in *A Treasury of Russian Spirituality*, ed. G. P. Fedotox. New York: Macmillan, 1966.